What Others Are Sayin

This book provides practical t(
Get it, read it, use it, and don'ı
continuing source of great ideas.
George Morrisey, Author, Morrisey on Planning series

Open this book to any page and you'll be impressed with the many practical strategies. Kristin's advice and insights have greatly increased our teams' productivity and success.
Jim Morton, Team Leader, Cubic Applications, Inc.

If you are sincerely interested in the continuous improvement of teams, read this book. It will move your team from "stall" to "speed" on road to success.
Marlene Caroselli, Director, Center for Professional Development

Team Basics provides user-friendly tips that will give even the novice the required skill and tools to be an effective leader, member, or facilitator. I highly recommend it!
Steve M. Hays, Chairman, Gobbell Hays Partners, Inc.

In *Team Basics,* I found page after page of quick insights and techniques that will smooth the team's work and assure better results.
Floyd Hurt, Author, Rousing Creativity

Kristin's dynamic book on team basics provides you all the information and encouragement you need to create a "team extraordinaire"!
Carol A. Dennis, Manager, Executive Development, T. Rowe Price

If you implement just a few of the ideas in this book, you will see tremendous personal, professional and team growth.
Ray Kniphuisen, Leadership Instructor, Northeast Nuclear

Team Basics is a one-of-a-kind book on teams. It is clear, easy to reference, and to the point. It is a book every team member should have, and I guarantee it will not sit on a shelf somewhere with all the "theory" books.
Barbara A. Glanz, Author, CARE Packages for the Workplace

Thank you so much for putting all these helpful nuggets together in an easy to use format.
Debbie Mollura, President, Creative Gifts Galore

Team Basics is the kind of book that becomes dog-eared and coffee stained from frequent use. Unless you're a fan of learning everything the hard way, you will enjoy it.
Denise M. Chicoine, Founder, Women's Business Exchange

If you have this book, you will no longer feel powerless when working in a team that isn't going anywhere.
Mark S. A. Smith, Co-author, Guerrilla Negotiating

This is a "must read" for anyone who serves as a team leader, manager, or supervisor. This book will assist you, save you time, and make life easy and fun as you plan and conduct meetings with those you work with.
Kae Kindle, Educational Specialist, Henrico County Public Schools

Team Basics is a "must have" for anyone who works with teams – facilitator, team member, or team leader. It is a gold mine of tips and tools guaranteed to help you and your team be more effective and successful.
Karen Lawson, Author, The Art of Influencing

Team Basics is filled with insightful tips to motivate you and your team members to communicate and work closely together in order to achieve SUCCESS.
Joanne R. Handyside, CPA, Failes and Associates

Kristin condenses her wisdom into highly accessible form for the use of anyone who has a team to form and run. It is a must-own for team leaders and members.
Thomas I. Young, Associate & Director of Specifications, SHG Inc.

Teams that don't practice these basic principles are certain to waste everyone's time (best case) or paralyze the organization (worst case). Use this book to help your team achieve its potential.
Robin Lawton, Author, Creating a Customer-Centered Culture

Team Basics is a primer of management tools for the 21st Century and a blueprint for organized solutions.
Bob Cole, VP Business Development, POMOCO Auto Group

Team Basics is an outstanding, no-nonsense guide packed full of tools, tips and techniques that work. It is a must for anyone trying to increase effectiveness of meetings and improving his or her skills as a team facilitator or leader.
Steven Holcomb, Internal Consultant, Newport News Shipbuilding

TEAM BASICS

Practical Strategies for Team Success

Kristin J. Arnold

QPC Press
Hampton, Virginia

TEAM BASICS
Practical Strategies for Team Success

Kristin J. Arnold
Copyright © 1999
All rights reserved

Printed in the United States of America
First printing 2000
Library of Congress Catalog Number: 99-96068
ISBN: 0-9676313-0-0
Library of Congress Cataloging-in-Publication Data
1. Business
2. Teams in the Workplace

Published by: QPC Press
48 West Queens Way
Hampton, Virginia 23669
800.589.4733
www.qpcteam.com

Cover Design: Marnie Deacon Kenney
Interior Illustrations: Dom Renaldo

Disclaimer

Table of Contents

Foreword

It is impossible to pick up a magazine or a newspaper without reading a report about a company that has doubled its productivity, increased efficiency fivefold, decreased error rates, or increased profits by 50%, all due to — you've got it — teamwork.

Consistently producing superior services and products has been the key to shaping successful American organizations. The foundation for meeting this challenge has been an increase in organizational teamwork. Teamwork is an asset few organizations can afford to be without.

What comes to mind when you hear the word teamwork? Positive thoughts such as working together, achieving common goals, and having fun? Negative thoughts including too time-consuming, personality clashes, and difficult communication? Both positive and negative thoughts occur because you've probably experienced both. There is nothing as exciting as being a member of a team that has efficiently, pleasantly, and successfully achieved its goal. On the other hand, nothing is more demoralizing as being a member of a team that is inefficient, stressful, and ineffective — whether it achieves its goal or not!

As we look to organizations of the future we will see more: *more* teams, *more* individuals working on *more* than one team at a time, *more* kinds of teams, and teams handling *more* responsibility and *more* complex issues. Teams will include *more* customers and suppliers. Teams will be *more* virtual, *more* cross-functional, and *more* dynamic than ever.

Why? Change is occurring too rapidly for one person (e.g., a manager) to know everything about every issue, with total accuracy, all the time. The only alternative is teamwork. It looks as though teamwork is here to stay. That's the good news.

The bad news is that it is always difficult to move an organization to a teamwork orientation. In fact, changing a traditionally management-centered culture to a team culture is asking an organization to do the opposite of what it has done in the past.

The individuals in a team-oriented organization must accept the responsibility for making their teams work. Teamwork may not be natural for everyone, especially those who have spent most of their working lives in a traditionally management-centered organization. Teamwork may not be natural for many if us. Why? Because most of us were brought up to do the best we could as individuals.

Even now, in all but the most progressive organizations, most employees are rewarded according to how much they accomplish as individuals, not as good team members. For example, have you ever been rewarded for helping someone else, even though it meant you didn't accomplish your own goals? It takes a different way of thinking. It may take a different way of acting. And it takes some new skills, or at least some concentration on skills we may have, but don't always use. And that's where this book can be a great resource for you.

Whether you are a manager, team leader, team member, or facilitator; or if you are an external consultant, trainer, or contractor, you will find this practical guide offers ideas and techniques to make a demonstrable difference in the performance of your teams. Kristin's tools and techniques have been used with every kind of team imaginable. All benefit from her sound advice, wise suggestions and years of experience. You will, too!

November 1999   Elaine Biech, author
                                 The Business of Consulting

Preface

This book was written with you in mind — to give you great information that you can put into use *immediately*. Whether you are a team leader, facilitator or team member, you will gain some practical tools and techniques to increase your team's effectiveness.

As a master facilitator, team trainer and national speaker on the topic of teams, I ask people *just like you*: "What's working and what's not working in your teams?" "What have you learned?" "What do you need to know to be successful with your teams?"

As I worked with these teams, I captured the responses, lessons learned and sage advice in my bi-weekly column aptly entitled "Teamwork."

This book represents the work my clients and faithful readers have found most valuable and helpful. It's about the *basics*. What you need to know *now* that will help your teams *now*. It's chock-full of hard-hitting, practical advice.

Use this book as a quick reference guide. Flip through the pages. Discover one new idea or "golden nugget" that will help your team work better!

I am pleased to offer *Team Basics* to anyone forming a team, leading a team or participating on a team. Enjoy cruising through these pages, discovering better ways to work together as an extraordinary team!

December 1999   Kristin J. Arnold
                                                  Hampton, VA

Acknowledgements

I can't say enough about the people who have helped me write this book. You have been my inspiration and my support to make this goal a reality. I am immensely grateful to:

The Reading Public who avidly read *The Daily Press* every other week, searching for tips and techniques to help their teams become extraordinary. You call or e-mail with questions and concerns. Without you, I wouldn't know what to write.

The Daily Press **Business Editor**, Mike Toole, who so graciously agreed to my idea for a bi-weekly column on teamwork (even though he couldn't fathom how much I could possibly write on teamwork!).

The Coast Guard Reserve Quality Team (RQT), the model and inspiration for many of the ideas in this book. Without our incredible, wide-ranging team experiences, I wouldn't have a clue about what it takes to be extraordinary.

My Clients who are so supportive and encouraged me to make this book a reality. You gave me confidence that the business world needs this book.

My Family and Friends. My ever-so-patient husband, Rich, and my two wonderful children, Travis and Marina, and my incredibly talented and insightful sister, Joy Stasiak.

My Editor and friend, Elizabeth Felicetti. Her talent with words is remarkable. This book would be a mess without her.

Thank you all for your wonderful help and support as I grow and develop *The Extraordinary Team*.

Introduction

Are you part of a team? If you play on a sports team, work with a bunch of people, or simply come together for family dinner...that's a team! Whenever you bring two or more people together for a desired outcome, you have a team.

All of these teams have an equal potential to be an extraordinary team — a high performance team that accomplishes the desired results quickly, efficiently and effectively. An extraordinary team has the following characteristics:

Clear Goals. Everyone understands the purpose and direction of the team. Everyone pulls in the same direction for success.

Shared Roles. Team task and maintenance roles are clearly defined and easily shared between team members.

A key shared role is the team leader. The "leader" shares the responsibility and the glory, is supportive and fair, creates a climate of trust and openness and is a good coach and teacher. The leadership role shifts at various times and, in the most productive teams, it is difficult to identify the leader during a casual observation.

Open and Clear Communication. Poor listening, poor speaking, and the inability to provide constructive feedback can be major roadblocks to team progress. For success, team members must listen for meaning, speak with clarity, engage in dialogue and discussion, and provide continual feedback through the communication process.

Effective Decision Making. The team is aware of and uses many methods to arrive at its decisions. Consensus is often touted as the best way to make decisions — and it is an excellent method — but the team should also use command decision, expert decision, majority vote, minority control, and command decision with input. Depending on the time available and the amount of commitment and resources required, a successful team selects the appropriate decision making method for each decision.

Valued Diversity. Members are valued for the unique contributions they bring to the team. A diversity of thinking, ideas, methods, experiences, and opinions is encouraged. Whether you are creative or logical, fast or methodical, team members recognize each other's individual talents and tap their expertise — both job-related and other skills they bring to the team. Flexibility and sensitivity are key elements in appreciating these differences.

Conflict Managed Constructively. Problems are not swept under the rug. Some may compete to have their opinions heard, while others may accommodate the stronger team members or avoid the conflict altogether. A successful team has discussed its philosophy about how to manage conflict and sees well-managed conflict as a healthy way to create new ideas and to solve difficult problems.

A Cooperative Climate. The atmosphere encourages participation, trust and openness. Members of the team are equally committed and involved. They know they need each others' skills, knowledge and expertise to produce something together that they could not do separately. There is a sense of belonging and a willingness to make things work for the good of the whole team. People are comfortable enough with each other to be creative, take risks and make mistakes. It also means you hear plenty of laughter and the team members enjoy what they are doing.

This book will take you through the process of creating and building an extraordinary team.

Chapter One

Set Your Team Up For Success

Wouldn't it be great if every team was an extraordinary team? They all can be...and the first and most important step is make sure the team is set up for success. If you are the team leader or sponsor of the team, this chapter is written specifically for you. You are ultimately responsible for creating a solid foundation for the team to do great work.

If you are a team member or facilitator, it is your responsibility to *ensure* you have a solid foundation. Ask good questions to make sure that each of the key elements described in this chapter are in place.

Once everyone has a clear understanding of why the team was put into business, the team can move forward quickly.

Start slow...to move fast!

Are You Ready for Teams?

If you are serious about moving your organization from a traditional, hierarchical organization into flexible, nimble teams, think through the benefits and costs—as well as the many cultural changes that you, your employees and customers will have to face. For some, the changes are just too great, and teams may not be the best solution. For many, the benefits far outweigh the disadvantages.

Any organization interested in moving toward a team-based environment should have:

A Sound Business Reason. More than just the program of the month, the company has a core strategy that teams will deliver the products or services better, faster and cheaper to the end customer. Teams are typically used to solve tough problems, improve wasteful processes, increase customer satisfaction, or strengthen the organization.

A Ready Culture. The climate within the company is ready for teams. People already cross traditional boundaries to get work done. They work well together and all indicators point toward "teaming" as a better way to achieve results with a higher degree of quality and commitment.

A Defined Approach. Before you decree that everyone should be on a team, think through how you will use teams over the long run. Some companies prefer the "amoebae approach" where the right people come together to work on a project for a limited period of time. Others prefer a more structured approach where people form into logical process teams, based on the products and processes that they provide to internal and external customers. Or people come from various parts of the organization to work on a specific problem or task. Whatever you do, don't put people on teams just because they sit close to each other! They MUST have some work in common.

Leadership In Front. The company's leadership (that means you, buddy) or leadership team (you and your direct reports) needs to be actively involved. Be more than just supportive or "behind" this initiative. Be in front! Kick off the training and activities. Pop in to a team meeting. Be genuinely interested in the team's progress. Recognize and reward teamwork. Personally make sure the teams have whatever they need to succeed.

Start Small. Begin with a few teams working on important processes that can have a high impact on the bottom line. Pick your best and brightest people to be on the initial teams. Once you have some tangible results, it'll be a lot easier to "sell" the team concept to the skeptics and cynics. You'll also learn what works well and what needs improvement.

Team Charter. Put the team in business with a formal charter that spells out your expectations. The charter should speak to the duration, checkpoints, boundaries, resources required, guidelines and logistics of the team. Always have a challenging (but not unreasonable) quantifiable goal (e.g. percent reduction in cycle time) so the team can measure its progress.

Training. Working in teams requires a different set of skills than working independently. Give the team the knowledge and skills to be successful and to assume the various roles required.

Patience. Try not to micromanage the teams. If you have a strategy in place, a solid charter, and interested and trained team members, let the teams do great work. Just like anyone learning to walk, your teams will stumble and fall. Be patient, support them and coach them to achieve the team's goals. Over time, they will become the nimble, flexible teams that will take your business to the next level.

To Team or Not to Team?

Teams are not the panacea for all your organization's ills. Just because your company has adopted a team approach, not everything must be accomplished by teams! Many tasks and challenges are best handled either by an individual working alone or by a small sub-group from the main team. Where appropriate, bring the right people together when the issue is:

Complex and requires expertise from a variety of disciplines. One person doesn't have all the information or answers.

Non-linear. The work occurs simultaneously and many different tasks, functions and people are linked together.

High Stakes. The problem or opportunity area affects more than a few individuals, and people have a big stake in the issue.

High Commitment. The business results will require a high degree of involvement and commitment in order to develop and implement the solution.

Teams are *not* appropriate when there is:

No Time. You may not be able to form a team when there is an immediate, full-blown crisis. (But you can let others know what you did after the fact.)

Expertise. One person has the knowledge and resources to accomplish the task. In addition, that person should have the power and authority to implement the decision with or without others' involvement, support and commitment.

No Support. If the organization doesn't support the team efforts, don't even bother with the team approach. For example, if management isn't open to the team's suggestions, won't provide the resources, or can't accept the team's recommendations, you're doomed.

No Common Ground. Team members have no work in common — or if they do, it is clearly not the team's main line of business.

Just because you put people on a team together doesn't mean they are going to act like or work like a team. It may make perfect sense to continue treating team members as separate individuals, rather than artificially trying to weld them into a more cohesive team unit. The challenge is to divert work to where it is best accomplished. Not everything has to be tackled as a team issue.

One other note for those of you jumping on the team bandwagon: teams don't really "do" work. Teams are great at discussing, planning and agreeing (or disagreeing) on what to do, but the physical and intellectual work still must be performed at the individual level.

So, if you find yourself spending over 50% of your time in meetings, you have been sucked into "meeting mania." Take a good look at where you are spending your time. Ask: Is this meeting necessary? Is there a better way to help us achieve our goals? Do I have to be present? Are we making substantial progress on achieving our goal? Are we following the rules for effective meetings?

Benefits of Teamwork

So you're still not quite convinced teams are a sound work strategy? Or you're trying to convince some stalwarts of the benefits of working together as a team? Organizations that effectively use teams can expect to see increases in productivity, service, quality, employee morale, and reduction of overhead, among other things. A high performing team can:

Do the Unthinkable. They can solve problems that have stumped the expert; improve broken processes that have been a major source of waste and rework; implement plans that couldn't be done. Because they are creative and synergistic, effective teams can save your organization between three to ten times their cost in time and support.

Go Where No Man Has Gone Before. Teams break down the boundaries or "silos" that separate functions within your organization. Teams create interactions between diverse people, both horizontally (across functions, processes, or even organizations) and vertically (up and down the organization — from the "big banana" to the front-line employee). Teams get people talking, learning, and taking action together.

Be Fast and Flexible. Teams can be more responsive to changing customer needs and a competitive environment. A team of people with the right skills, resources and direction can come together quickly to achieve great results.

Make Things Simple. Teams can take a challenging, complex project and sort out the details and problems. Rather than placing the load (and the blame) on one person, everyone shares the burden *and* the rewards.

Make Better Decisions. If one person has all the answers, you don't need a team. But two (or more) heads are better than one. When you have more than one person thinking about a problem or issue, ideas flow and creativity sparks. New possibilities are generated. And when implementers are part of the decision-making process, they are much more committed to a successful outcome.

Hug Each Other. There are emotional benefits in having teams — even if some of us don't like to admit it. Teams provide a sense of belonging, helping people appreciate where they fit and how they contribute to the organization's goals. When working as a team, people support and encourage each other, understand each other better and communicate more effectively.

Still don't believe? Recognize the benefits to you, the individual working within the team. In a well-run team, you can expect to be part of the decision-making process, sharing responsibility and rewards. Team members often have higher morale, less stress, greater involvement, commitment, self-esteem and job satisfaction, and a shared sense of accomplishment and camaraderie.

Charter for Success

Before assigning a group of people to work together as a team, the sponsor or "champion" should think about why the team needs to be in business and what they will need to set them up for success. The sponsor is typically the person in the organization with the clout to make the team's recommendations a reality - and the courage to let go of the team details.

One of the ways they can "let go" is to create a team charter: a written description of what the team is being asked to do, including the scope and constraints. The sponsor and team leader should work together to build the charter, which typically contains the following elements:

Background. Give the reason(s) for chartering the team. State the perceived problem/project and any information that would be useful to the people who must complete the project.

Mission, Vision or Goal. What you, the sponsor, or the process owner (the person with the most at stake to win or lose in the process/project/problem) wants from the team. What the team is expected to do and what changes are expected as a result of this teamwork. Beware: If you are vague about your expectations, don't be surprised by what the team finally delivers!

Membership. Choose your members carefully. Volunteers are best, the process owner a must. Make sure you have representation from every key part of the process as well as from different levels within the organization. Consider using a facilitator to keep the team on track and to provide training as needed.

Duration. How long the team expects to work on the project. Intact work groups are perpetual; task forces, process improvement, and problem solving teams have a finite life span—typically no more than six months or they lose steam and wither away.

Checkpoints. When you expect the team to check in with you. At the very least, the team should check in at critical times during the project.

Feedback Mechanism. How the team communicates with you, the people they are representing and other members on the team.

Boundaries. Any issues that are "out of bounds" and not for the team to consider.

Resources. What resources (money, training, specialists, support, equipment, supplies) will be needed.

Guidelines. Any specific areas to address, processes to be used, people to involve or whatever you think needs to be considered in order to accomplish the team's goal.

Logistics. When, where, how often, and for how long the team will meet. How the team members' "normal work" will get done while they are involved on the team.

Once the team members have been identified, the sponsor should bring them all together to discuss, agree with, and modify (if necessary) the team charter. Once you have agreement on the direction, scope and process, the team will be in a much better position to move forward quickly and successfully.

Vision and Mission

Many teams get confused over the difference between mission and vision. So let's start with some simple definitions:

The Mission defines your team's core purpose or reason-for-being as concisely and clearly as possible. The mission is the foundation for all of the team's efforts. It defines what the team does, and more importantly, defines what it *doesn't* do.

Vision, on the other hand, is the team's declaration of its future. Vision is a long-term, over-arching team goal. The vision typically states:

❑ What and where the team wants to be—a vivid description of the most desirable future.

❑ When the team wants to achieve this—usually three to seven years in the future.

A well-crafted vision paints the picture of the preferred future and can energize a team to move forward in a unified direction. It should excite and inspire the team so all team actions can support the expressed vision.

Quite simply, a mission describes what business your team is in. It defines what you do. Vision describes where you are going.

Can they be merged? Yes, it is possible that a mission can be stated within a vision, and a vision can be stated within a mission. Regardless of what you call it, there are some great reasons why teams should spend some time defining what they do (mission) and where they are going (vision):

❑ It provides a sense of purpose and direction to the team.

❑   It helps to distinguish your team from others
    and describe your team's uniqueness.

❑   It gives your team a starting point for defining
    its strategies, goals and structure.

❑   It becomes a basis for making critical and daily
    decisions.

Is it worth the time to define the mission and
vision? You bet. Otherwise, you have a bunch of
individuals working on their own goals and agendas.
Just don't get bogged down in terminology. A
statement or statements about what you do and where
you are going is the "glue" that holds the team together.

Unfortunately, many teams agonize over mission
and vision, "wordsmithing" the statements until they
are perfect. In the meantime, it drains all the energy
from the team!

When crafting your mission and vision, let the team
contribute the main thoughts, words, phrases and
insights, and then let a few volunteer team members
wordsmith the statement "off-line." This will save the
entire team time and energy, and the team members
will remain positive and upbeat about their purpose
and direction.

Team Mission Statement Examples

To improve the welding process by 40% from the moment
we receive the part to the moment it is delivered to our
internal customer.

Process Improvement Team

To provide human resource solutions by being informed
consultants helping to meet our company's mission and
vision.

Intact Work Team

To successfully manufacture a new product with the first
shipment out the door to our primary customer by 6p.m.
June 30 of this year.

Project Team

Set Team Goals and Milestones

Teams need focus and direction either through a vision or goal statement. An all-encompassing vision or simple, well-defined goals provide the team with a unified sense of what is important. To set clear team goals and milestones:

Agree on a Time Frame. Three, six, nine months or a year are good time periods. I like to use holidays as the endpoints: New Year's Day, St. Patrick's Day, Fourth of July, Labor Day. Then you have two reasons to celebrate!

Brainstorm. "What should we have accomplished by then?" Ask each person to write each idea on a separate stickie note. Remind the team that all ideas are valid. After a few minutes, ask the team to call out its ideas and place all the stickies on a flipchart.

Sort Silently. Ask the team to move the stickies into clusters of similar items — without talking. If you disagree with where someone puts a stickie, simply move it! Within a few minutes, the team has quickly organized the brainstormed items into three to seven categories.

Create a Header. For each category, ask the team to create a "header" — a word, phrase or statement that captures the essence of all the stickies in that category. Sometimes, an "odd ball" doesn't quite fit. That's okay — the team can move it to another category. When finished, write all the "headers" on a new flipchart.

Look at the Big Picture. Take a moment to look at the new header flipchart. Do the headers make sense? Has your team covered all the main goal areas? Should some headers be combined?

Create a Goal Statement. Take each header and create a SMART goal statement which is Specific,

Measurable, Achievable, Results-oriented, and Time-dimensioned. A good format to use is "We will be/have/become (a specific result) by (date)."

Identify Major Steps. From your stickies, identify the major steps to achieving each goal. Go through a "sifting" of the brainstormed items: Does the item contribute to achieving the goal? Does it come before or after the other major steps? The result is a linear timeline of what needs to be done to achieve the goal.

Assign Responsibility. For each goal and major step, ask for a team member to be responsible for completing that step. Spread the wealth so no single person has the load.

Identify Resources. Resourcing can be an issue for more complex plans. For each major step, identify what resources (time, people, money, equipment, material) will be needed. Look for the linkages (two-fers and three-fers) where the same major step occurs in two or three goal areas. These are your high-leverage activities. In some cases, the timeline will need to be adjusted or the costs will simply outweigh the benefits.

Follow Through. Now that you have your plan, just do it! Periodically come together and review the status of your plan. Congratulate yourself on your successes and modify if necessary. Remember, the planning process is just as important (if not more so) than the plan itself. Slow down and plan it right so your team can implement the plan and take advantage of opportunities which complement the plan and help the team achieve its goals.

What Type of Team Are We?

We all approach teamwork with our own notions about what makes a team. Our past experiences both cloud and clarify our views. When you find yourself on a team, ask yourself a fundamental question: "What type of team are we?"

Teams come in different shapes and sizes based on the direction, membership, task, participation, duration and location of the team members:

Direction can come from management or from within the team itself. In a controlled team, management selects the assignment, defines the process and closely monitors the activities. A guided team receives assignments and suggested methods from management, while a self-directed team selects its own assignments and methods.

Membership can be intact or cross-functional. People from the same department or division generally form an intact team. People from different departments, divisions or levels within the company form a cross-functional team. A customer-supplier team expands the membership to other players upstream or downstream from the team's product or service.

Task can be creating, planning, implementing or coordinating. Creation teams generate ideas and directions; planning teams coordinate the success of the idea; implementation teams carry out the plan. Your team may have one or all of these tasks to accomplish.

Participation can be either mandatory or voluntary. Ideally, you want to have volunteers, but sometimes you must "select and direct" participation of key individuals with essential knowledge or skills.

Duration can range from a short time to a long life. Temporary teams are formed to handle specific projects, to solve a problem, improve a process, innovate a system or implement a plan. Once finished, the team disbands. A permanent team has continuing responsibility for an area or situation. It looks at a variety of issues that are related to a broad, long-term goal. Once the team has finished with one issue, it tackles another.

Location can be in the same place or dispersed to several locations. Members of a dispersed or "virtual" team are expected to perform as a team even though they are separated in space and time. Geographically dispersed or "virtual" teams can take advantage of the diversity of different cultures and points of view.

Obviously, there is no best type of team. Teams are meant to be flexible, dynamic and creative structures which support the organization's strategy and objectives. However, unless the unique features of the team are defined and agreed upon by team members, different agendas and expectations may pull the team apart.

Team Types

Direction	Participation
❏ Management	❏ Voluntary
❏ From Within	❏ Mandatory
Task	**Membership**
❏ Creation	❏ Intact
❏ Planning	❏ Cross Functional
❏ Implementation	❏ Customer/Supplier

Duration

❏ Short   ❏ Medium   ❏ Long

Select the Right People for Your Team

You need the right people on the team in order to be successful. This may seem obvious, but many teams fail because the person with the money, control or interest wasn't part of the process. Whether you are trying to solve a problem, improve a process, implement a decision, plan a strategy or achieve a specific result, you need people who:

Know Their Stuff. The process owner or subject matter experts (SME) who know the technical side of the issue or process.

Know Process. Facilitators know how to get from the current state to the desired state using process tools and techniques.

Touch the Process. Include those people (or representatives) who impact the process along the way. They have a good sense of what is going on, where the pain is and what to do about it. They are usually the "make or break" people during implementation.

Can Make a Decision. This criteria is often the fatal flaw of many cross-functional teams. One person represents a department but does not have the authority or influence to make a decision for that department.

At this point, you have at least four people on your team (unless you have a "two-fer" — one person who wears two hats). Try not to have more than ten people on a team. A cozy number of core team members is six to eight people. You may decide to bring in other team members on an "as needed" basis. The key is to let them know you may need them to participate and keep them informed of your progress. Then you won't have to spend a tremendous amount of time bringing them up to speed. Consider including:

A Customer. If possible, include one or two of your best, worst and/or average customers of the team's product or process. Encourage these customers to think "strategically" in that they are representing all of your customers. If you can't fathom having customers on your team, at least allow their voice to be heard. Designate at least one person to "check back" with customers, test ideas, and bring customer data.

A Supplier. If your process is dependent on inbound products, raw goods or information, you may want to consider inviting your key supplier(s).

A Specialist. Maybe your team is going to need to survey a population, statistically analyze data, or construct work breakdown structures for a project plan. If your team doesn't have the skills to do this, get help! Bring the "expert" to the team — not necessarily to do it for them, but to show them how to do it. Now those team members will be able to transfer those learned skills to other teams!

Once you have identified the right positions on the team, make sure you have the right mix of people:

Volunteers. It's always better to have people who want to be included in the process rather than prisoners.

Diverse Strengths and Abilities. A team is greater than the sum of its individual parts. So make sure you have a "big picture" person as well as one who is detail-oriented, fast paced, slow paced, etc. You are striving for the right combination of people to complement each other and build on each others' strengths.

Team Skills. Working in a team requires new skills and behaviors. It is always easier if there are some seasoned veterans with positive team experiences and skills. Because they believe in the team's potential, they raise the entire team's standards and expectations.

The Team Launch

Your first team meeting sets the tone for the rest of the project. Typically, the "Team Launch" consists of the following elements to ensure success:

Define the Team. In *The Wisdom of Teams,* Jon Katzenbach defines a team as "a small number of people with complementary skills who are committed to a common purpose, performance goals, and approach for which they hold themselves mutually accountable." Discuss why this team was formed and how the team will work better than a single individual.

Get to Know Each Other. Start with introductions and a team activity. Keep it upbeat and tied to the team's overall objectives. Some may get impatient with this "fluff" but, the better team members know each other, the more willing they are to trust each other. Without trust, a team cannot work together.

Review the Team Charter. Most teams are chartered by management to accomplish a specific goal or produce a tangible deliverable. Review the charter elements which include background, the goal, membership, duration, critical milestones or checkpoints, boundaries, logistics and resources required. Be prepared for all kinds of questions — and when you don't know something, say so! Some things might be open for discussion; others are "off limits." Let the team know early on which is which.

Team Charter Checklist

☐ **Background**
The reason(s) for chartering the team. State the perceived problem/project and any information that would be useful to those who must complete the project.

☐ **Goal or Deliverable(s)**
What the sponsor and/or process owner wants from the team. Clarify team expectations and what changes are expected to result from this teamwork.

☐ **Membership**
Representation from every key part of the process as well as from different levels within the organization.

☐ **Duration**
How long the team is expected to work on the project.

☐ **Checkpoints**
When you expect the team to check in with the sponsor. At the very least, the team should check in at critical milestones.

☐ **Feedback Mechanism**
How the team communicates with the sponsor, the people they are representing and other members on the team.

☐ **Boundaries**
Any issues that are "out of bounds" and not for the team to consider.

☐ **Decisions**
Most teams aim for consensus, with a fallback to the team leader or majority vote.

☐ **Resources**
What resources (money, training, specialists, support, equipment, supplies) will be needed.

☐ **Guidelines**
Any specific areas to address, processes to be used, people to involve or whatever else needs to be considered in order to accomplish the team's goal.

☐ **Logistics**
When, where, how often, and for how long the team will meet. How the team members' "normal work" will get done while they are involved on the team.

Go Where the Work Is. Take a tour of the actual physical location where the work will be performed, put together, used or delivered. Seeing the space and talking to the end users of the team's product builds more understanding and commitment to the team's goal.

Expose the Process. Create or let the team know the overall process, how the team will accomplish its goal and how decisions will be made. Is the team really aiming for consensus — a decision everyone will live with and support upon implementation? Or are they making recommendations for management to decide? How will the team be making their own internal decisions? Command decision? Loudest voice? Majority vote? Consensus? Unanimous?

Clarify Success. Make sure the team has a clear picture of success. Is it reduced cycle time? Increased customer satisfaction? Producing an error-free report? Implementing a project within time and cost constraints? Ultimately, they need to know what "success" is. Having a clearly defined target helps keep the team on track and enables the team to celebrate achieving their goal.

Agree on Ground Rules. When people come together as a team, they go through a predictable pattern of behavior: form, storm, norm, and perform. It is perfectly natural to have your ups and downs — just don't get stuck! Agree on some explicit ground rules about how the team will work cooperatively together and how they will manage the inevitable conflicts.

Agree on Meeting Rules. Where there are teams, there are meetings. Vow to follow these core meeting rules: use agendas; have a facilitator; take minutes; enforce your team ground rules; draft your next meeting agenda before you leave; critique the meeting to improve your team work.

Housekeeping. There are usually some logistics and support issues that must be addressed: supplies, meeting room reservations, percent of time devoted to the project, parking, etc. Remember, the little stuff bugs people, so pay attention to the little stuff early on.

Communicate Regularly. Discuss how the team will communicate progress internally and up the food chain. Agree on intended audience, purpose, method, frequency, format and location.

Remember, as you launch your team, you won't be able to dot every "i" and cross every "t." Be authentic and genuine in your desire to work together as a team toward the same goal. Teamwork is built over time, and this is the first and most important step in setting your team up for future success.

Develop a Communication Strategy

At this point, you have made a strategic decision to use teams to achieve specific business results. It's important that you communicate the progress and results appropriately throughout the entire organization.

To develop an organization-wide communication strategy, use a small, cross-functional team representing all elements, including your public relations people and:

Identify the Target. Who are you trying to communicate to? Who needs to know and/or be motivated about these teams?

Assess the Needs. For each target group, identify what they need or want to know. Talk to some of the members of each group and test your assumptions. When establishing teams:

❑ Declare the business case for teams.

❑ Share the vision for team work.

❑ Reinforce the organization's core values.

❑ Model teamwork in establishing your communications strategy.

❑ Be open to interaction, constantly improving the process.

❑ Acknowledge that mistakes can happen. And when mistakes *do* occur, be timely, open and honest in your disclosure of the information.

Prepare the Messages. Draft the content of what you want to communicate to each group. Be clear and consistent while tailoring messages for each target group.

For example, senior managers usually respond to top line (revenues) or bottom-line (net income) results;

middle managers may want to know about operational efficiency; and employees could be more interested in how this will make their workday easier.

Again, test your messages with each group. Messages are likely to be misinterpreted. Make sure they are clear and understood.

Select Media. Examine your current communication vehicles. Are they sufficient to carry the messages? If not, this may create an opportunity to establish new communication patterns. Perhaps integrate technology with e-mail, intranet, voice-mail, closed circuit television, videoconferencing.

On the other hand, don't defer to technology just because it is easier to send out an e-mail. Select the appropriate media.

Originate. For each group, decide how you want to send the message out (all at once to everyone or cascaded down through the "food chain").

Sequence the Messages. Decide how often the messages should be communicated and through which medium. Messages need to be repeated in various forms. Remember the adage: You have to tell someone something three times before they actually comprehend what you said.

Don't Overload. Watch out for information overload with too much detail, or too many messages saying the same thing the same way.

Listen. Employees will always read between the lines and invent the worst picture possible. Be open and accessible. Listen to their fears. Share additional information if you can.

Ask for Feedback. Set up simple feedback mechanisms to measure your success. What effect do you want your communication to have? How will you know if you have been successful? Based on the feedback, adjust your strategy accordingly.

Beware of the "Rock Phenomenon"

The "rock phenomenon" occurs when the boss asks the team for a "rock." The team delivers its version of the rock—something different from what the boss expected. So the boss says "wrong rock" and tells the team to search for another rock—with little or no guidance.

*"I didn't mean I wanted **that** rock..."*

To avoid the "rock phenomenon," the boss should clearly articulate his or her definition of a job well done, the desired outcome(s), and any other functions and features required in the end product. The boss should take time to explain the reasons for asking for input, any parameters or constraints, as well as how the decision will be made. Is the boss simply getting team input and then making the final decision? Or is the team aiming for consensus where the boss is but one voice and the team agrees to live with and support the decision? The key to a consensus decision is that anyone on the team (including the boss) has an opportunity to voice an opinion.

Keep in mind that if the team cannot come to a consensus, then the decision will fall back to the boss (or a majority vote). Don't worry, the boss still has input and if push comes to shove, the final say. Over time, the team will trust that their ideas are truly valued and are important to achieving a team consensus.

Recognize that it takes courage for a boss to open up and ask for input. The boss may not like what is said and may feel compelled to justify each comment. And the team may feel uncomfortable being open and honest. So watch out for the "dashboard dog" effect when everyone on the team just repeats what they think the boss wants to hear.

The best thing a boss can do is actively listen. Try not to judge and evaluate what has been said. Then add your idea as one among all the others. Challenge others to discuss the issues openly. And don't punish them for speaking up.

Chapter Two

Plan A Successful Session

Meetings have become an integral part of the day-to-day operations of most organizations. Often viewed as a necessary evil, they can account for a significant number of hours in your business day. Regardless of whether or not you like them, these marketplaces for ideas represent an excellent opportunity to share opinions, resolve conflicts, and build solutions to tough problems.

This chapter will focus on the process you *should* go through to plan for a successful team session. Unfortunately, most teams and organizations still call a meeting at the drop of a hat — with obvious poor results.

According to a study by the University of Southern California:

❑ The average meeting is attended by nine people notified two hours prior to the session.

❑ It has no written agenda, and its purported purpose is completed only 50 percent of the time.

❑ A quarter of the participants complain they waste between 11 and 25 percent of the time discussing irrelevant issues.

❑ A full third of them feel pressured to publicly espouse opinions with which they privately disagree.

❑ Another third feel they have minimal or no influence in the discussion.

Planning Sheet

Overall Goal

Purpose

Desired Outcome(s)

Deliverable

Scout the Context

- [ ] Individuals
- [ ] Team
- [ ] Organization
- [ ] Industry

Team Roles

- [ ] Team Leader
- [ ] Facilitator
- [ ] Recorder
- [ ] Timekeeper

Create the Environment

- [ ] Lighting
- [ ] Location
- [ ] Refreshments
- [ ] Room Layout
- [ ] Technology
- [ ] Temperature

Decision Strategy

- [ ] Aim for Consensus, Fallback to...
- [ ] Expert
- [ ] Majority Vote
- [ ] Minority (Loudest Voice)
- [ ] Team Leader
- [ ] Unanimous

Process

- [ ] Generate
- [ ] Organize
- [ ] Select
- [ ] Take Action

Ground Rules/Preventions

Build and Distribute the Agenda

Plan a Successful Meeting

The success of your team session is directly proportional to the amount of planning you have given it. In order to plan for a successful meeting, follow these steps:

State the Overall Goal. Almost every meeting is part of a series of meetings related to an overall organizational goal.

State the Purpose of the Meeting. Given the overall goal, define the purpose of the meeting. For example, to provide or gather information, plan an activity, solve a problem, make a decision, share information or take action.

Identify the Desired Outcome(s). What do you expect to accomplish by the end of this particular meeting?

Identify the Deliverable. Given the desired outcome(s), what tangible deliverable do you want as a result of the meeting? For example, an action plan, a list or an agreement.

Scout the Context. Every meeting takes place within a greater context. Scout the environment to determine which events have an impact on the meeting. Notice how the meeting may affect other events. Examining the context helps avoid larger surprises.

Determine Team Roles. Spread the wealth and get others involved by giving other team members a role in the meeting. Identify the team leader, facilitator, timekeeper, scribe and/or recorder. Ensure each team member has a clear understanding of his or her duties and responsibilities.

Create the Environment. With a bit of forethought, you can create a good meeting environment given the constraints that all organizations face. You can reserve the room, sit in a U-shape, have all the "working stuff" already on the tables (e.g. stickie notes and markers). If the meeting is longer than two hours, have some refreshments. Even ice water is a nice touch.

Select a Decision Strategy. State up front how the decision will be made, whether it is a command decision, expert decision, majority vote, minority control, command decision with input or consensus. Describe how the decision will be made, by whom, who will be involved, and how they will be involved.

Select a Process to Achieve the Outcome. Identify how you are going to accomplish your objective. For example, you might brainstorm, review, list or discuss a topic.

Build the Agenda. Take all of the above and build your agenda, listing the amount of time, the topic, the process, and the "leader" of that piece of the meeting.

Distribute the Agenda, preferably at least 48 hours prior to the meeting.

A Typical Team Agenda

A typical team agenda has the following key elements:

Time. An estimate of the amount of time each section will take. Try not to keep it too global, nor too specific. Remember, the timekeeper will be holding the team accountable to these times, so estimate wisely!

Topic/Task. A list of the topics and/or tasks the team wants to cover.

Process. A best guess at the process the team will use to achieve the task. Most teams go through a typical process of generating ideas, organizing those ideas, selecting or making a decision, and then taking action.

Presenter. The team member who will lead the team through that particular topic. The presenter may (or may not) be the team leader. Extraordinary teams share the wealth and allow all team members to lead the team through different topics.

On the next page, there is a template that you may use to build an agenda.

A Sample Agenda

Date _____ Location _____
Title _____
Purpose _____
Desired Results _____
Team Leader _____ Recorder _____
Facilitator _____ Timekeeper _____
Team Members _____

Time	Topic/Process	Presenter

Open the Meeting
  Review/Revise Agenda
  Establish/Review Ground Rules
  Team Activity/Ice Breaker

Content
  Topics/Process to Be Used

Close the Meeting
  Review Key Understandings
  Review/Clarify Actions Required
  Set Next Meeting's Agenda
  Critique the Team's Work

Build an Agenda from Scratch

When there is no agenda, ask the team to build one! Before the team gets too involved in spinning its wheels, put your hand up and ask, "Where's the agenda?" If the other team members look at you with glazed eyes or eager expressions, take advantage of the situation.

Quickly hop up out of your seat, grab a flipchart marker and ask:

"What Do We Need To Accomplish at This Meeting?" Ask the team to identify specific outcomes or expected results. Write down each idea *the way it was stated* and the name of the person who suggested the idea.

Before you move on to the next step, ask if everyone understands the outcomes and clarify if necessary. Combine similar items. If there is any dissent, assume that the ideas are distinct and should remain separate.

Keep up the momentum by referring to each item and asking each suggester two questions:

"How Long Will It Take to Achieve the Outcome?" If the team disagrees, allow a few seconds for discussion and write down an estimated time. Remember: an agenda is just a road map, and the time limits are guideposts. If the team later agrees that it needs more time, it will have the flexibility to adjust the agenda.

"Would You Like to Lead the Discussion?" If not, ask the team for a volunteer. Beware: if just one or two people are leading all the items, you will end up with a one-way conversation!

Prioritize the List. Most teams have too much to do and not enough time, so it is critical to start with the most important. Some teams simply rank the agenda items with number one being the most important, two as the next most important, etc. Or try the ABC method:

- ❑ "A" is vital — we *must* accomplish this outcome at this meeting.

- ❑ "B" is important — we *should* accomplish this outcome.

- ❑ "C" is trivial — we *could* do this, but the world won't come to an end if we don't accomplish this today.

When prioritizing, quickly go through the list and ask "Is this an A, B, or C?" and write down the most popular letter. Some teams continue to prioritize by sequencing each group of letters — identifying A1, A2, A3, B1, B2, B3, C1, C2, C3.

You have now built your agenda in just a few minutes — a worthwhile investment to the team's work! Start with the A1, and move to A2 and proceed through the list.

Create the Environment

The way your meeting room is set up is one of the most important factors in determining your meeting's success. It affects the team members' comfort, receptivity, attitude, and degree of involvement.

As you prepare for your next meeting, consider:

To Sit or Not to Sit. If you are having a "quickie" meeting (less than ten minutes), keep them standing. If you are going to sit down, sit in a U-shape or semi-circle. Flipcharts can be placed at the opening so all members can focus on the task at hand. Team members can see each other and discussion is encouraged.

Table It. Consider having a meeting with no tables or barriers to communication — just people talking to people.

Not Too Big, Not Too Small, but Just Right. Have just enough space so team members aren't crowded. Not too large that the empty chairs and space suck all the energy out of the room.

Seats, Everyone. If your meeting will last over an hour, take a look at the chairs. Wheels on chairs are nice, armrests are good, extra padding is great. Otherwise, schedule breaks often!

Something to Drink? Water on the tables is a nice touch and costs nothing. Coffee and juice in the morning and sodas in the afternoon as well as snacks are a real treat. Donuts are a classic meeting food but include a healthy alternative such as bagels or bran muffins. In the afternoon, try cookies, cheese and crackers, or a vegetable tray.

Location, Location, Location. Have the meeting centrally located, so that no one participant is inconvenienced. The room should be close to the restrooms and a public phone. The entrance/exit doors should be at the back of the "U" so participants are not interrupted.

Paraphenalia. Flipcharts, pens, pencils, markers, note pads and stickie notes are useful during most meetings. If you can, use your company's imprinted items — they add a great boost to the team's morale and remind everyone of the organization's common goal.

Lighting and Temperature. Know how to adjust the lights and temperature. If you know that the location is usually at "Ice Station Zebra," advise the participants to bring a sweater.

Technology. Overhead projectors, LCD panels, copyboards and notebook computers are being used more frequently. Will someone need the technology on site? Who will bring it, does it work, and is there electrical access (three-prong plugs and extension cords)? Whatever your plan, do a dry run. Whatever can go wrong will go wrong.

Visit the room prior to the event. Make sure it is the best possible environment. Run through the agenda and ask yourself, "Is there anything I can do that will enhance the team members' contributions?"

Attention to these small details can make the difference between a dull, unproductive meeting and one that is upbeat, enthusiastic, and really gets results.

Last Minute Checklist

Arrive a few minutes early to set the stage for success:

Post the Mission. On a flipchart or poster board, write the team's mission or goal statement on the wall for all to see. This serves as a reminder of why the team was created.

Have an Agenda. Hopefully, all team members have already received a copy of the agenda. Just in case, make copies for each member or post it on the wall.

Arrange the Tables. If they have not already been set up, move the tables and chairs into a "U-shape." The entrance to the room should be at the base of the "U" to limit any distractions from people coming or going. Place any visuals (e.g. easels, whiteboards or projector screens) at the opening of the "U," so all can be focused on where the action is!

Check Your Gadgets. Remember Murphy's law: what can go wrong will go wrong. Have a back-up ready, just in case.

Make Handouts. If you are going to be referencing other material, make sure you have copies for everyone. You will lose momentum if one person is discussing statistics or information that no one else has seen or has access to.

Stock the Meeting Kit. Keep some meeting supplies handy in a basket or plastic container. You'll be glad you did, especially when your marker runs out!

I always keep my facilitator's kit handy. It's a black tote bag full of goodies such as:

- ❏ Advil®
- ❏ bandages
- ❏ correction pen
- ❏ masking tape
- ❏ marking pens
- ❏ mounting putty
- ❏ name tags/tents
- ❏ paper clips
- ❏ Post-it® flags
- ❏ Post-it® notes
- ❏ Post-it® correction tape

- ❏ push pins
- ❏ rubber bands
- ❏ scissors
- ❏ Shout® wipes
- ❏ stapler
- ❏ stick pins
- ❏ straight-edge ruler
- ❏ Tic-tacs®
- ❏ transparencies
- ❏ transparency pens
- ❏ watercolor markers

Greet Others. As your team members enter the room, don't forget to smile and say hello!

Where Should You Sit?

You walk into the room a few minutes before the meeting begins. You check out who is already present and where they are sitting. You grab a cup of coffee and sit down at the first available seat. Or do you?

People choose their seats for all kinds of reasons. Some sit wherever there is an empty seat. Others want to sit where they always do. Some want to sit next to a particular person. Others want to be close to the coffee pot.

Select your seat to increase your success in achieving your objective:

Power. Sit at the end of the table.

Influence. Sit directly across the table from someone you want to influence. This provides maximum opportunity for eye contact, verbal and non-verbal messages.

Leadership. Although most meeting leaders typically sit at the end of the table, the best place is in the middle seat on either side of the table. This allows the leader more flexibility to control the conversation or "gate-keep."

Build Trust. Sit to the right of a person when you want to generate a feeling of trust. In medieval times, people of questionable loyalty were seated on the left because right-handed people would normally thrust a dagger to the left! Hence, we now have the term "Right-Hand Man."

Alignment. Sit next to (preferably to the right of) the leader or other individual when you want to be identified with that person. This puts you in view as people look at the leader, and a subliminal connection is made.

Attention. Sit directly across from or next to someone you want to have notice you.

Discussion. Choose the "central seats" (those at the ends and the middle seats) when you want to be actively involved in the meeting discussion. Don't sit next to the leader who is acting as "gate-keeper." The leader will recognize you _less_. If you want to stay out of the discussion, choose the corner seats.

Confrontation. Sit directly across from someone who has an opposing view or recommendation.

Networking. Sit next to anyone with whom you want to strengthen your relationship.

Exit. Sit closest to the door in the event you must leave before the meeting is over or if you want to make a quick exit.

Comfort. When you don't have a compelling reason for choosing one seat over another, sit wherever you are most comfortable!

Kick It Off!

The first few minutes of your team meeting set the pace and tone for the rest of the session. You only get one chance to make a first impression, and your team is looking to you for leadership, guidance and support. What you say and how you say it create a climate that contributes to the success or failure of the team.

Here are a few tips to set your team up for success:

Countdown. "We're going to start in two minutes." Then, start on time.

Capture Their Attention with a smart move to the front of the room or head of the table.

Begin with Confidence. Kick it off with a team "icebreaker:"

❏ Start with an anecdote — share a personal experience that would be understood by all. Make it relevant and genuine.

❏ Use an imaginative visual — weekend comic strips or editorial pages. Don't forget to check your copyright laws and, if necessary, ask permission to use the artist's work.

❏ Ask a rhetorical question to stimulate thinking on the topic.

❏ Give a unique demonstration or example.

Discuss the Purpose of the meeting, provide background information, and explain the team's value to the organization. Review the team charter or mission, if there is one.

Introduce Yourself and your role on the team. Allow others to introduce themselves and describe their experience, expectations and/or reservations.

Agree on the Approach, Agenda, and Activities. Show how each individual expectation, meeting purpose and agenda correlate. Check for understanding and agreement.

Clarify Expectations for team involvement: e.g. attend meetings, take notes, do homework, read material, conduct research.

Explain the Evaluation System. Let the team know if they will have an opportunity to critique the team's work and its performance as well as how the overall team will be evaluated.

Agree on Ground Rules, logistics and other administrivia. Some typical examples might include agreements on start and stop times, breaks, how decisions will be made and who will take notes.

To ensure success, keep your comments upbeat and focused. Discuss each point and move on to the next item on the agenda. Don't allow your comments to drag. Show the team that they are in good hands and that you are well-prepared. They will then be able to put aside some of their concerns and focus on the team's work.

Agree on Ground Rules

Every meeting should have some ground rules — explicit agreements on how the team will function. Ground rules should be established or reviewed at the beginning of each meeting, before getting down to business.

As you formulate your ground rules, consider how the team is going to deal with common concerns such as:

Interruptions. What to do when members are called out of the meeting. How to deal with phone calls and messages. Will pagers and cellular phones be tolerated?

Assignments. If members cannot complete their "homework," who should they notify, and by when?

Roles. Should the team rotate roles? Which ones and how often? In the event a team member can't make it to the meeting, are "substitutions" allowed?

Decisions. How will the team make its decisions? Are the members aiming for consensus? Is there a "fallback" in case the team can't come to a consensus? Is the team leader making the final decision?

Confidentiality. Are there topics or kinds of information that should not be discussed outside the meeting?

Penalties. How will the team deal with minor and chronic violations of the ground rules?

Ground rules are to teams as the Constitution of the United States is to America. Ground rules provide a solid foundation to the values of the team. They clearly state what is important to the team and what members can expect from each other. As the team evolves and matures, the ground rules will change, creating "amendments" to the team's constitution.

Ground rules are simply the glue that holds the team together. Some ground rules ideas:

Honor Time Limits. Be on time. Start on time. End on time. Set a time frame on each team deliverable. Do your part to meet individual and team commitments.

All Participate...No One Dominates. Ask for ideas from everyone. Recognize and consider others' ideas. Accept all suggestions as valid for consideration.

Work Together. Team members communicate and work closely together and make every effort to support one another. Work together to solve problems. Offer help without being asked. Keep each other informed.

Listen as Allies. Give your undivided attention to the person speaking. Seek first to understand, then to be understood. Respect each other by not interrupting. Stay on track. Stick to the subject at hand. Minimize distractions and debate.

Be Considerate. Consider the needs, motivations and skills of other team members when offering help or advice. Be open to constructive feedback.

Celebrate Small Successes. Recognize team *and* individual effort.

Knock Three Times. Simply knock your knuckle or a pen on the table three times if the discussion starts to wander or there is another minor violation of the ground rules. Whoever is speaking should stop and refocus on the topic.

Respect Time and Each Other.

Break the Ice

An icebreaker or "warm-up" is a wonderful technique to start a meeting. If done properly, these team activities create an energizing environment, enhance the team's work, get people talking and acquainted.

Some people love to start with icebreakers, while others want to dive right into the content of the meeting. So when you do warm-ups, follow these guidelines for success:

Make It Quick. Especially the first few times you do a team activity, make sure it lasts no more than five minutes. If your meeting is more than an hour long, you can increase the time accordingly.

Involve Everyone. Make sure the activity has everyone actively involved. This means no wallflowers — everyone has something to do or is expected to contribute in some way.

Make It Okay to Pass. Some people may not want to participate — for whatever reason. In the introduction, tell your teammates they can say "pass" if they don't want to participate.

Tie It to the Team. Most folks will go along with the activity if it has some relevance to the team's work. Introduce the icebreaker, why you chose that activity and what the benefits are — especially if the activity is a game or is unusual.

Start Out Easy. Many teams start out with an easy icebreaker where a question is asked and then each team member answers the question. For example: "Share with us the best team you have ever been on" and then each member answers the question. Stay away from "getting to know you/what's your hobby" perfunctory questions that add little value.

Keep It Lively. After the team has done a few easy icebreakers, try a different type of activity. There are dozens of books on icebreakers, warm-ups, team activities, games, etc. that may inspire you to try something different. If you want to encourage flexibility of mind, look for imaginative or creative activities.

Be Prepared. Bring instructions, handouts or supplies with you.

Enjoy Yourself. If you are looking forward to the warm-up, then others will too.

Thank Them. At the conclusion of the activity, thank everyone for participating, and continue with the agenda.

After a while, the team will expect these icebreakers and you can experiment with the length, content, and different methods. Encourage other team members to bring in new team activities and build the team! You'll find that team members learn from each other what they like and dislike, what works and what doesn't, and how they work together as individuals and as a team.

Chapter Three

Share Team Roles

The next time you go to your team meeting, take a few moments to observe the team functions and roles. At any particular moment, someone is leading, taking notes, keeping on-track and on time, as well as participating in the meeting. Watch closely who is performing each function.

The team leader may be working very hard at *all* of these functions — not only leading the meeting, but keeping notes on a yellow legal pad, steering the agenda and the timetable, and answering questions without a whole lot of participation.

This chapter will encourage you to "share the wealth." Stop working too hard, and let other team members take responsibility for team functioning and success.

Share Team Roles

If your team leader is "sharing the wealth," you may see many team members performing some basic team roles:

Leader sets guidelines, helps to establish goals and leads specific parts of the meeting.

Recorder keeps the visual memory of the team, capturing the nuggets of information so that all can see and follow the team's progress. At the minimum, the recorder captures key subjects and main points raised, decisions made and items that the group has agreed to raise again later.

Facilitator guides the team process — helping the team understand the issues, reach agreements and plan next steps. The facilitator keeps the meeting on the topic and focused by opening and closing discussions, managing participation, providing process tools and techniques, checking for decisions and intervening when necessary.

Timekeeper keeps time as established in the agenda and ensures that the meeting does not run overtime on any particular subject. The timekeeper provides warnings when time is running out.

Team Members contribute to the team, share their knowledge and expertise, participate in all meetings and discussions, and carry out their assignments between meetings.

In an extraordinary team, team members freely volunteer and often informally assume these basic team roles to ensure effective team functioning. The sharing of these roles and functions encourages team involvement and participation.

If you see only one or two people taking care of all the team functions, you may want to introduce this concept of sharing team roles. Suggest that different team members volunteer for each of the roles. Be clear about the definitions of each role and then conduct your team meeting.

At the end of the meeting, take a few minutes to check the process. Ask: "Did the roles help the team?" and "What could we do differently?" Reinforce what went well, and improve on the "do differentlys" at the next team meeting.

The Team Leader

The team leader is the most pivotal role on the team. The leader sets the tone and expectations for how a diverse group of people will work together to achieve specific results.

The team philosophy may be new to some team leaders and members. They will instinctively continue to work independently and look to the leader for specific task direction. To build productive teams, team leaders must direct, guide, facilitate, and coach.

Leading teams means making tough decisions to obtain the appropriate level of involvement, calling upon the experience and expertise of each team member. Strategies vary according to the maturity of the team — spending more time directing at first, and then developing and evolving to the point where the team can handle more and new responsibilities and work *interdependently*. As you build your team:

Tell 'Em Everything. As you set the team up for success, clarify expectations, guidelines, deliverables and deadlines. Be willing to state what you know — *and* what you don't know. The team needs to have the same information you have in order to build trust and work together.

Be a Coach. The successful team leader coaches the team so it can be more involved in preparing and planning the work, knowing what work is being done, and setting high performance goals. Of course, this means that you may need to bone up on coaching and team dynamics. Find a great team facilitator to train and coach you!

Watch Process as Well as Content. Be concerned not only with what the team does, but how the team goes about its business. You can't achieve great results over the long term without also focusing on what is happening to and between team members.

Share the Wealth. Traditionally, the team leader "leads" the team (and does most of the talking), records what's being said on a yellow legal pad, and keeps time (or forgets to watch the time and everyone is stuck for an extra two hours....). Why not share the wealth? Ask for different team members to be the recorder, timekeeper or even "lead" different parts of the meeting.

Don't Hog Airtime. Watch how much "airtime" you use. Do you dominate the discussion? Are you the first or last to speak? Do you offer your opinion? Ask for advice? Ask others for their ideas?

Be Part of the Team. You put your pants on just like everyone else. You are no better nor worse than your team members. So check the ego at the door and look forward to doing great work with great people.

Aim for Consensus. The most common concern I hear from team leaders is the fear that the team will march off in a direction the leader thinks is unwise or inappropriate. When the team aims for consensus, *that will never happen.* Think about it. Consensus means that all can live with and support the decision upon implementation. If you, as a team member, can't live with it, then you don't have a consensus!

Have a Fallback. If the team gets jammed, and can't reach a consensus (or they possibly could, but will talk longer than you have time for), then "fall back" to a previously identified position. For example, many teams declare "We will aim for consensus, but in the event we cannot reach a consensus within this meeting, we will fall back to 'the team leader decides'." Someone has to break the "tie." In this case the team leader calls it. Or you can fall back to a majority vote.

Select Your Team Leader

The team leader is the primary point of contact between the team and other parts of the organization. The team leader acts as the spokesperson to higher levels of management and resolves conflicts between supervisors and managers.

Management typically appoints the team leader if the team is just forming and members don't know each other well. In a few cases, management doesn't yet have a high degree of trust in the team's decision-making process and therefore finds it necessary to appoint a leader at the onset. They typically appoint the process expert or senior member to lead and represent the team at management briefings.

Management must choose an individual who has demonstrated facilitative leadership skills, or they should be prepared to train the prospective team leader. The team leader should be well-respected by the team and other stakeholders, be technically competent and have the best interests of the team and the overall organization in mind. Some organizations use an assessment instrument or a simulation to forecast how well the potential team leader will interact.

The Team may decide who the team leader is going to be. Typically, teams select the obvious "leader," (most senior, most knowledgeable, most outgoing etc.), but for management to be truly comfortable with the team decision, the team should decide its leadership based on specific criteria as mentioned above. In this way, management will feel more comfortable and confident with the team's decision.

It is not unusual for an informal leader to emerge mid-way through the team development process. The informal leader usually complements the formal leader's spokesperson role by ensuring open and clear communication, cooperative relationships and effective decision-making.

Rotating Team Leaders volunteer or are assigned the leadership role for a specific task and within a specific length of time. This ensures balanced participation and allows team members to learn new leadership skills and sharpen their team skills.

Set some ground rules on how the role will rotate:

❑ Will everyone rotate into leader role?

❑ For how long?

❑ Will any additional training be needed?

❑ Will responsibilities change depending on the leader's knowledge, skills, and abilities?

❑ For self-directed teams, will there be additional compensation?

All teams need a team leader to focus the efforts, set guidelines, and deliver results. How you go about selecting your team leader depends largely on the mission, management, organizational culture and development of your team.

Recorder Captures Key Information

Want your teams to stay focused? Capture and post key information on the wall — on flipchart paper, whiteboard or the blackboard. Your team members will stay focused and on track as well as remember and act on the information well after the meeting.

Some kinds of information you might post include:

Meeting Purpose. The mission, goal or objective of the meeting.

Agenda. The chronological sequence of events or list of items to be discussed in the meeting. Include who will lead the discussion and the timeframes.

Ground Rules. Agreed on team norms that guide the effective functioning of the team (e.g. honor time limits, don't interrupt...).

Team Map. This could be a timeline, schedule, flow of events, project plan or process map.

Parking Lot. Make stickie notes available to your team members to "park" items that need to be discussed or done in the future or a comment to the group without taking up valuable airtime.

Action Plans. All teams should have an action plan chart where tasks and deadlines are noted and assigned.

Capture information while the team is talking to ensure understanding and clarity of what has been said. For instance, if an issue was broken down into four parts, capture those four parts on an overhead transparency (more than 15 people) or a flipchart (fewer than 20 people) or on a blackboard (small classroom). This serves as a reminder of what has already been said and agreed upon.

Easel on the Wall

Leave your easel behind and create an easel on the wall! Take your easel pad and place a piece of tape on each of the bottom outside edges. Lift up the sheet of easel paper. On the second sheet, place a piece of tape on the bottom edge, just inside of where you place the tape on the top sheet. Continue to place the tape so five sheets of paper can come down off the wall one at a time.

Take all five sheets in hand and rip the sheets off the easel pad, all at one time. As a nice, neat stack, tape your "pad" on the wall!

TAPE UP SEVERAL STACKS OF PAPER

STAGGER TAPE SO SHEETS CAN COME DOWN ONE AT A TIME

USE ABOUT 5 SHEETS PER STACK

HAVE EXTRA STACKS READY TO GO UP.

Tape up several stacks of paper, depending on how much wall space you have. Or have extra stacks ready to go up when you need them.

Fantastic Flipcharts

Recording ideas, key points, agreements, decisions, and action items is a great way to keep your team focused and on track. When using flipcharts:

Write in Large Capital Letters. Use the thick part of the flipchart marker. Leave a margin on both sides of the chart.

Capture Key Words the speaker uses. Abbreviate where possible. If you miss a point or don't understand, ask for the speaker to repeat or clarify what was said. If in doubt, check with the team members to see if you captured the idea correctly. If you aren't sure how to spell a word, ask for help. Or have a ground rule that missspelling is okay.

Let Everybody See. Stand to the side of the easel when not writing. The point is to capture ideas so team members can use their combined thoughts to move forward. Post charts on the wall with masking tape or low-tack tape.

Use Color. Alternate between two colors with each new point. Use dark colors such as black, brown, blue, dark green, or purple to record the team's ideas. Highlight key points with orange, yellow or pastels. Keep in mind that some people might be color-blind!

Be Bold. Emphasize titles with underlines, clouds or pictures. When listing items, bulletize with circles, diamonds, boxes or arrows, not with numbers. Number each page and post on the wall so all can see.

Have Tape Ready. Before the meeting begins, stage extra pieces of masking tape on the easel or edge of table so that you can quickly post the flipchart paper. Place the tape vertically on the top, about one inch from each side rather than at a corner angle. This will allow for easy removal. If posting on expensive wallpaper, use a high quality drafting tape.

When you take down the paper, turn the tape over onto the back of the paper — this will keep the tape from sticking to other sheets.

Be creative and have fun recording your teamwork! Use colors, pictures, and symbols to express your team's thoughts and energy. If you don't consider yourself to be artistic, try using "wingdings" or trace a picture from clipart or a coloring book.

At the end of your meeting, agree on what information needs to be saved, and in what format. Some teams simply roll up the flipcharts and post them right before the next meeting. In this way, they are ready to start where they left off. Other teams like to type up the key points and action items as "meeting minutes" and distribute them shortly after the meeting. Still others have electronic copyboards which immediately reduce the flipchart into letter-size paper which is handed out as the team members leave the room.

Effective Facilitation

The facilitator is a formal role with the primary responsibility of guiding the team toward its goal. A facilitator focuses on the process (the "how to") rather than the content (the "what" the team is addressing). While there are plenty of content experts on the team, it is the facilitator's job to make sure they get to where they need to go as efficiently and effectively as possible.

As a facilitator, some of the key activities you need be involved in are:

Clarify the Charter. Get together with the sponsor and team leader and make sure you (and they) understand the team's goal(s) and expectations, the composition of the team, timeframes, deliverables, capabilities, and constraints.

Partner with the Team Leader. Before the team ever meets, get together with the team leader and agree on the basic strategies to move the team forward. Some team leaders will need lots of support and coaching from you. Others will have a good sense for how to proceed. Regardless, you must meet with the team leader to ensure you are on the same sheet of music. Agree on how you will prepare for and critique each meeting. Develop an initial agenda for the team to follow. Agree on a "cue" to signal to each other when you should adjust the strategy or take a break to confer.

Keep on Track. As the process expert, you provide structure and process tools to help the team achieve its goal. At the beginning of each meeting, ensure the team agrees to the agenda and time limits. Keep the meeting on the topic and moving along.

Intervene when Necessary. When the team gets off track or if the discussion fragments into multiple conversations, you must step in to bring the team back on topic.

Manage Participation. Open discussions and invite participation. Tactfully prevent anyone from being overlooked or dominating the discussion. Summarize and close discussions.

Check Decisions. Teams make small decisions throughout the meeting. When you sense a decision has been made, check for understanding and agreement. Make sure the team understands the next steps and who will do them.

Develop the Team. Your secondary goal is to enable the team to function effectively without you. This means that you are constantly training, coaching and developing the team leader and team members. Initially, you may be very active and involved in all aspects of the team's work. As the team matures, many of your responsibilities will be assumed by other team members. In a high-performing team, the facilitator role is shared among team members, and a designated facilitator may no longer be required.

If you prepare correctly, most of your work will be done in the planning, preparation and debriefing of the meeting. The actual "facilitating" of the meeting becomes a small part of your involvement. A long-term measure of your success is that you are not required to intervene during the team meeting. The team facilitates itself.

Terrific Timekeeper

The team should agree on how it will manage its time during the meeting. The timekeeper keeps time as established in the agenda and ensures that the meeting does not run overtime on any particular subject. The timekeeper provides warnings when time is running out.

The timekeeper should provide warnings as time is running out. For instance, if twenty minutes is allocated to discussion of a particular topic, the timekeeper might warn the group at the ten minute mark, the five minute mark, the one minute mark and then signal the group when time is up.

When the time is up, the team may decide to:

Continue. Renegotiate the timetable and continue the discussion. (Remember, meetings start and end on time).

Close. Move toward immediate closure of the discussion.

Park It. Save the issue for another meeting.

Team members enjoy working together

Team Members are Team Players

The best team players constantly share the spotlight, making sure everyone has the opportunity to shine. They pay attention to others before focusing on themselves. They offer help without being asked. They do things because they need to be done, even if it isn't their "job."

In my experience, these kinds of teams are truly extraordinary. They enjoy working together to achieve success. There is an atmosphere of mutual respect and consideration of others.

This type of teamwork doesn't happen overnight. It starts with a few people setting the standard and the ground rules for team cooperation. Over time, other team members adopt these behavioral norms until they become second nature for the team.

Try these techniques to build an extraordinarily cohesive team:

Praise Works Wonders. Look for the good in each team member and recognize his or her contributions to the team. Compliment their efforts, achievements and good qualities. Recognize the simple things they do, such as being on time, completing assignments and other tasks that may be considered "just part of the job."

Be a Cheerleader. Constantly encourage others to do their best work. Support them through the good and not-so-great times. Even when they don't succeed, note that they tried their best. When ready, help them try again.

Be Considerate. Think of the Golden Rule: Do unto others as you would have them do unto you. You can see this principle in action in the little things they do: asking others for their opinions, being attentive, actively listening, validating what others have said, not interrupting or having side conversations.

Focus on Others First. Truly care about others and how you can help them be successful. You'll be amazed that what goes around, comes around.

Think Win/Win. You have to believe that there are enough "wins" to go around. If you think there are enough wins, you don't have to compete with your fellow team members! By working together, everybody succeeds.

Share the Glory. When the team achieves a critical milestone or goal, give credit to each team member. Recognize that one person couldn't have accomplished the task alone, and that the team is greater than the sum of its parts.

Team Champion

Every team needs a champion or sponsor, a higher level manager (or a group of managers) with a stake in the team's performance and results. The champion acts as an advisor to the team leader, supports the team and removes roadblocks to achieving the goal. Ultimately, the champion's primary role is to ensure the team's success — not necessarily to "do" the team's work.

Champion(s) should have a stake in the outcome, the ability to influence or the authority to make changes, the ability to delegate, the clout to remove barriers *and* the courage to trust the team.

If you don't know who your champion is, go get one! Your champion was probably involved in bringing the team together, chartering the team, or selecting most of the team members. A champion is your advocate "up the food chain" and can often venture where team members dare not go.

The champion is NOT an active member of the team. There is a tendency for many champions to dig into the weeds, getting involved in the day-to-day tactics of the team. Agree up front on your roles and how you will keep your champion apprised of the team's progress.

As a champion, your team expects you to:

Show Support. Attend *some* (but not all) of the meetings. Know everyone's name. Be positive and enthusiastic. Talk up the importance of the team's activities and progress throughout the organization.

Kick It Off. Be present at the very first team meeting. Communicate your personal perspective on the importance of team success. Explain the reasons why the team is being chartered and what is at stake if the team does or does not succeed. Clarify your expectations and describe "success." Express your commitment to follow through on the team's decisions and recommendations.

Know Stuff. Learn about the team's progress through staff meetings, e-mails, voice-mails, and office chatter. Be the team's eyes and ears. Alert the team if you hear anything good or bad.

Pave the Way politically and financially to ensure team success. Be an advocate for resources. Make sure the right connections are made for the team's recommendations and decisions to be supported through implementation.

Intervene on behalf of the team. Sometimes, the team can't speak for itself. Someone "up the food chain" must speak on its behalf. Speak with the same passion and commitment as the team.

Recognize Performance. At key milestones and when all is said and done, make sure the team and its members are recognized for a job well done.

Define Roles and Responsibilities

As your team comes together, it is important to define the roles and responsibilities beyond the sharing of team roles. Most people want to know where they belong on the team — why they are there and what is expected of them. Take the time to clarify their roles. Ask team members to share their:

Expectations. Ask what they expect from the team and how they might be able to contribute to the team's success.

Job Description. Let team members describe, in their own words, what their job is, the work that they do, how they do it, who they work with and what they are responsible for.

Action Items. Clarify action items and responsibilities. Ensure team members have a clear understanding of what the task is, and what the team expects them to do. Agree on how the members will let the team know the task is accomplished.

Definition of a Good Team Player. Clarify the definition of a good team player. For example, he or she contributes meaningfully to the team, shares knowledge and expertise, participates in all meetings and discussions, and carries out assignments between meetings.

Balance Task and Maintenance Behaviors. Less tangible, but just as important, is the team's interaction skills. We all think we are great team players, committed to getting the job done with others. An effective team demonstrates a wide range of task and maintenance behaviors:

Task behaviors enable the team to work on a specific task. Some task behaviors include:

- ❑ **Initiating.** State the purpose or objective. Offer opinion and ideas. Offer facts, examples or relevant information. Suggest a procedure or method for the team to follow. Suggest resource people to contact.

- ❑ **Asking.** Ask others for their opinions and ideas. Validate others' ideas. Ask others to clarify their opinions and ideas. Bring in others who may not speak. Poll the team for a consensus.

- ❑ **Clarifying.** Clarify or explain reasons. Provide concise examples and illustrations. Point out relationships between facts and opinions. Pull ideas and suggestions together.

- ❑ **Refocusing.** Refocus the team when joking, personal stories, or irrelevant talk goes on too long. Refocus the team by redefining goals, problems, or outcomes when things become hazy or confusing.

- ❑ **Summarizing.** Summarize progress or discussions. Summarize alternatives and issues facing the team. Celebrate small successes.

Maintenance behaviors ensure the team is working well together. Some maintenance behaviors include:

- ❑ **Encouraging.** Accept, praise and agree with the contribution of others.

- ❑ **Harmonizing.** Smooth out differences and relieve tension between team members.

- ❑ **Reconciling.** Search for common elements in conflicts. Get others to explain differences of opinion. Admit they could be wrong. Offer a compromise.

❑ **Compromising.** Constructively manage areas of disagreement. Aim to resolve conflicts by admitting an error, enforcing ground rules, or meeting others halfway.

❑ **Gatekeeping.** Manage airtime ensuring all participate and no one dominates.

❑ **Observing.** Observe group process and team dynamics. Provide feedback to the group to reinforce strengths and evaluate possible areas for improvement.

These task and maintenance roles can both help *and* hinder discussion. It's important to have a balance of all of these behaviors for effective teamwork.

Chapter Four

Work Through The Process

Your team should strive to reach decisions that best reflect the thinking of all team members. To accomplish this, teams go through a fairly typical process of generating ideas and organizing them to combine, synergize and select one or many to take action.

As the team moves through this fairly predictable pattern, the team makes small decisions in order to achieve a collaborative consensus — a decision that everyone can live with *and* support upon implementation.

Make Team Decisions

If your team is like most, it relies on two or three strategies to make decisions: consensus, team input with the team leader making the final decision, or the loudest voice wins.

Effective teams use many different decision-making strategies, depending on several key factors:

- ❑ The amount of buy-in necessary to support implementation
- ❑ How much time is available to make the decision
- ❑ How important the issue or decision is
- ❑ Who has the information or expertise needed to make the decision
- ❑ The developmental level of the team

Command Decision. The team leader or expert decides. Useful when a decision needs to be made quickly and the leader or expert is in control of the situation. Explain the reasons for making the decision to other team members as soon as possible.

Ask Individual Team Members, Then Decide. The team leader collects information from each individual and then makes a decision. Useful when you *cannot* assemble everyone in one place. Explain the criteria for making the decision, how each team member will be involved, and what type of input you need (ideas, suggestions, information). Be consistent in your questions and let the team know what you found out.

Team Input, Then Decide. By gathering the team together, you are creating opportunities for creativity, synergy, and buy-in. But this will take more time, and you may create conflict if you decide against the team's recommendation. The key is to explain the criteria for making the decision, how the team members will be involved, what type of input you want, and set a time limit for discussion.

Majority Vote is useful when the issue is relatively inconsequential or the team is stuck. Americans are pretty comfortable with a hand vote. Ensure everyone understands what is being voted on and the rules involved *before* the actual vote is taken.

Minority Rule or the loudest, most overbearing voice wins. This is usually the standard default for minor team decisions and inconsequential issues. It does, however, require a team member to have the courage to speak up with an opposing viewpoint.

Unanimous. The hardest strategy to achieve, *all* team members must agree on a specific position. This strategy is not recommended unless you *must* have all team members agree.

Consensus. Everyone can live with and support the decision upon implementation. For important issues where the team needs to educate themselves on the positions and issues, as well as implement the decision, most teams aim for consensus. The key is to explain exactly what consensus means — the team can and will not only live with the decision, but will support it upon implementation. Outline any constraints on the decision (time, financial, resources, political). Agree on a "fallback" strategy within a prescribed period of time, or you may never agree!

Regardless of which strategy you choose, every team member should know how the decision is going to be made and the guidelines involved.

Take a look at how your team makes decisions. Do you use a broad range of strategies, depending on the situation, or are you stuck using just a few? As a team, discuss how you might improve the ways your team makes decisions.

Brainstorm a List

Developed in the late 1930s by Alex F. Osborne to stimulate his advertising executives' creativity, brainstorming has blossomed across America's meeting rooms.

The ground rules are simple: All ideas are valid; to pass is okay; we'll continue until all pass; quickly capture ideas on an easel chart so all can see; adding to other ideas or "hitchhiking" is encouraged; no praise, no comments, no criticism.

There are three different methods typically used to brainstorm a list:

Freewheel. Anyone on the team can call out an idea, with one person capturing the ideas on an easel chart.

Round-Robin. The team leader goes around the table for each person to either contribute a new idea, add to, or "hitchhike" on a previous idea. Each person has the option to pass.

Slip. Each member writes down each of his or her ideas on a separate slip of paper, stickie notes or index cards. The ideas are then collected and organized.

If you are in the mood to experiment, try these variations on brainstorming:

Analogy. The team pretends it is solving a problem for a similar situation. The emphasis here is that it may be necessary to focus on a related situation in order to clearly understand the problem.

Compressed. Each team member writes down on a sheet of paper as many ideas as possible in fifteen seconds. When the team leader calls "time," each member passes the sheet to the left, and then has fifteen seconds to write down on the new sheet as many new ideas as possible. The key is to build on or enhance each others' ideas.

Idea Quota. The team comes up with a number of ideas in a predetermined timeframe. For example, twenty ideas in five minutes. The key is to come up with all kinds of ideas, then go through the list and pick out the ones that make the most sense to focus on.

Inversion. The team comes up with ideas destined to ensure the failure of the project or perpetuate the problem. The key is that good solutions can sometimes result from focusing on opposite goals.

Martian. The team comes up with the wildest or most "out there" ideas possible. The key is that wild ideas can be "tamed" to produce sensible solutions. One rule...any idea is fair game.

The final step to brainstorming a list is to clarify and combine similar ideas. Go through the list and ensure everyone on the team understands each item. Eliminate duplicates and combine ideas that are *very* similar. If there is disagreement on the team, keep the ideas separate.

Narrow the List to a Few

Your team has just brainstormed a creative, long list of ideas, solutions, problems, causes, or other items. Now what? Rather than simply roll up the flipcharts, toss them in a corner and forget them, you can take the next step and narrow down the list with a "quickvote."

Ten Votes. Each team member has ten votes. They can place all ten votes on one item or they can scatter their ten votes among the many items. Ask if anyone needs clarification of an item, or if any two items are so similar they should be combined. Clarify or combine, if necessary.

Silently Vote. Then ask each team member to silently vote by writing item choices and the number of votes on a piece of paper. To speed up this process, you may want to letter each item, starting with A, then B and so on down the flipchart. Then the team members simply write the letter and the number, e.g. A-3, F-2, H-2, I-2, L-1. Ask the team members to make sure they have "spent" all their ten votes.

Tally the Votes. Go through the list, starting with A, and ask the team members to raise the number of fingers for the number of votes they placed on that item. The recorder may then simply count up the numbers, or the members may choose to "sound off" in sequence by adding their numbers together. Write the total next to the item and take the vote on the next item until you have gone through all the items.

If privacy is an issue, ask the team members to write each of their items and the corresponding vote on small, separate stickie notes. For the above example, the team member would have five separate stickie notes. After all the team members have their votes written down, turn the flipcharts out of sight of the team, and ask each individual to come up to the flipcharts and place the stickies next to each item. Since this takes a bit longer, take a break after each team member has filed through and voted. The recorder simply pulls off the stickie notes from each item and adds them up! If a stickie note falls off the chart, it's easy to see where it belongs, since both the letter and the vote are written on the stickie note.

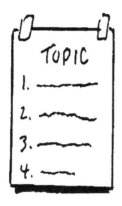

Reorder the List. Ask the team for the item with the most number of votes, and the next and the next. Capture the new list on a flipchart. You will see the list narrow down dramatically — at least by half.

There may be some vocal members who will want to take the top vote and declare it the "winner." Be careful — less than 50 percent may have voted for the "winner!"

A "quickvote" is used to narrow down the list, not to select a winner. If your list is really long, you may even do a few "quickvotes" (called a multivote) to narrow down the list to something manageable.

If the list is over 30 items, you may want to consider allowing the team members to have more votes — typically a third of the items. For example, if you have 51 items, then each team member would have 17 votes. Notice that it will be a bit harder and longer to vote and tally — especially if you have lots of team members!

When you have narrowed the list down to five or so items, see if there is a possible "consensus" in the mix of ideas. Is it possible to combine or create, or must the team select just one?

Voting Variations

The Simple Handvote. "Those in favor of option A, raise your hand...." While this may be the easiest and most familiar way to select one from many, it will divide your team into separate camps. There will be clear winners and losers — which goes against the spirit of teamwork!

Quickvote. Each team member gets 10 votes. They can place all 10 votes on one item or scatter them among many items. If you think the vote will be skewed with one or more people dropping all 10 votes on one item, call the 10-4 rule where one person can only put a maximum of four votes per item.

Multivote. The number of votes is a third of the total number of items. For example, if you have 12 items to choose from, each team member would have four votes. Like a quickvote, members can place all four votes on one item or scatter them among many items.

Nominal Group Technique. A rank order vote where each team member is required to vote for a third of the items. For example, if you have 12 items, you must vote for four items. The most important item gets a "four" (the highest number of votes possible), the second most important items gets a "three", the third most important number gets a "two" and the least most important number gets a "one." When you tally up the numbers, the item that receives the most number of votes is considered to be the most important. Also take a look at how many people voted for each item — you may find that just a few people voted for the top item.

If your list is really long (over 20 items), each of these voting techniques will only narrow down the list. Consider doing another voting round to ensure team buy-in and support of the final choice.

Selection Grid. If you must select between just a few remaining options, try the selection grid. List the options down the left side of the grid. List the criteria for selection across the top. Then evaluate each option against each criteria. If the option fulfills the criteria, place an "x" in the box. After the team has evaluated all the options against the criteria, see which option satisfies most of the reasons your team wants it!

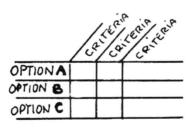

Before you call the vote, make sure everyone understands each option. Go through each item on the list and ask for the person who mentioned the item to briefly explain what the item means (no more than a minute for each item). As you go through this process, some items may be combined or even deleted from the list!

Then remind the team of the topic you are voting about. Ask the team members to individually make their choices and then call for the vote.

Sort Your Brainstormed List

Most brainstorming lists end up in a long-forgotten pile — usually because the list was too long or too intimidating to deal with. By organizing your brainstormed ideas, you can quickly sort your long list into a few manageable categories.

Clarify the Topic. Start your brainstorming session by clarifying the topic at hand. Write the topic on a flipchart for all to see.

Write Down Ideas. Ask team members to write their ideas on a 3 inch by 5 inch index card or stickie note. Each idea gets a separate stickie or card. Encourage them to write large and legibly. A great side benefit of writing each idea on a separate stickie or card is that team members get to write the idea in their own words and in as much detail as they like.

Sort the Ideas. When finished brainstorming, ask the team to sort its ideas. If they already have a sense for the general categories, then simply label several easel charts with the name of each category. Then ask the team members to place their cards in the appropriate category. Leave one blank sheet of paper up on the wall just in case another category emerges.

Hint: If using index cards, you can either spray the charts with adhesive spray, or write the categories on different colored index cards and work on a large table.

Sometimes, the team doesn't know what the main categories might be. In this case, ask the team to *affinitize* their ideas. In this process, place several sheets of blank easel paper on the wall. Then ask the team members to take each card and place it next to another card with a similar idea, an affinity or something in common. If the idea is exactly the same, simply put your card on top of the other. It's okay if you have a card that has nothing in common with the others!

The key to using the affinity diagram is that this process is done *without talking*. Once you put your card up on the wall, it is now the team's card. If a team member doesn't like where a card is, he or she can move it, rather than discuss it!

Make sure you have enough wall space for your team to sort through the ideas. You'll be amazed at how quickly the brainstormed list shifts from a huge blob into several discrete clusters. After the flurry of activity, give a ten-second countdown for all cards to settle into their clusters. Then label each cluster with a "header" that describes all the cards in that cluster.

Whether you categorize or affinitize, you get the same result — several categories or "headers" with several cards underneath each header. However, with an affinity diagram, you might see some non-traditional, even creative groupings of your ideas.

Now that you have organized that huge brainstorming list, your team may decide to prioritize the categories or "headers" to focus on one or two high priority categories. Or your team may decide to divide into sub-teams to look at each category in more detail.

Build a Consensus

Your team has narrowed a brainstormed list down to a few important items. In some cases, an obvious option leaps out and the team comes to a quick decision. Most of the time, however, the team is faced with a choice among many options.

If the team is interested and has the time, it can combine, create and synergize the items into a better idea. The team *builds* a consensus — striving to reach a decision that best reflects the thinking of *all* team members. Consensus means more than "I can live with it." It means that each team member can live with *and* support the decision upon implementation. To build a consensus:

Define "Consensus." Explain what consensus means and why it is important for the team to reach consensus. Ensure that all team members understand the issue and the most important items. To prevent confusion, take the time to define the specific meaning of the words being used. Clearly outline any constraints (e.g. time or money). Remind each member to participate fully in the discussion. Each person has an equal voice. Finally, identify a "fallback" if consensus can't be reached within a specified time (majority vote or command decision).

Ask Questions. Take the most important items from your brainstormed list, and ask a few probing questions:

❑ "All of these items are possible. Do we have to choose only one?"

❑ "Is there any way we can use the best features of each item?"

❏ "What would happen if we took added/deleted features of several options. Would that get us closer to what we want?"

❏ "Could we try out several options in parallel before we commit to just one?"

Team energy increases as new ideas and possibilities surface. This trial-and-error approach appears chaotic; however, the team builds a new, synergistic alternative based on the best of the best.

Straw Poll. When it appears the team has coalesced and agreed to a new alternative, take a "straw poll" — a pulse check to see how close or how far apart the team is from reaching a consensus. Remind the team that this poll is not a final vote — it simply tells them how much work needs to be done to build consensus. Try these sentence starters:

❏ "It sounds like we are making progress. Let's check that out with a quick straw poll to see how close we are to a consensus. We'll go right around the table. Sally?"

❏ "Let's see if everyone either can agree with, or can agree to support, the most popular alternative. Let's start with Sally and go around the room. Sally?"

❏ Or — try the "Test for Consensus."

Record the responses and summarize the results. If everyone can live with and support the alternative, then you have a consensus.

Build a Better Decision. Chances are that there will be some opposition, so find out what it would take to gain support. Try these sentence starters:

❏ "There seems to be a lot of support for this alternative. What would it take for the rest of us to support this?"

❑ "What is getting in the way of some team members supporting this alternative? What could we do to meet their needs?"

Continue to build agreement for the decision until you have a consensus, or time runs out and your team falls back to another decision-making method. By building a consensus, your team has a greater chance of producing a better quality decision, a more cohesive team and smoother implementation of the decision.

The Five "L" Straw Poll

Give each person a Post-It® Tape Flag. Draw the following "Five L" scale on the flipchart, describing each "L" as you write it:

"You loathe it, or hate it. You will lament it and moan about it in the parking lot. You can live with it — it's okay. You can like it. Or you can really love it."

Loathe   Lament   Live   Like   Love

Silent Vote. Ask the team members to silently identify how they view the proposed alternative. Then ask them to place their Post-It® Tape Flags on the item, so that they build a bar chart.

Loathe   Lament   Live   Like   Love

Consensus? See if the team agrees there is a consensus. Consensus is that all votes are at least a "live with" or better.

Build a Better Decision. In the event there are votes that are "loathe," "lament," or just a few "live withs," ask the team why someone voted that way. Be careful not to pick on a specific person, but get the team's feedback on why there isn't a consensus.

Action Plan Flipchart

Summarize your meeting by looking at and commenting on all the work posted on the walls!

Focus on the Action Plan chart and ensure understanding and agreement on the tasks, deadlines, and person(s) responsible.

Post the Action Plan chart on the wall at each session as a reminder of the commitments made.

Hint: Roll up the Action Plan chart inside out (so the print is on the outside). Unroll it and the chart will hang nicely toward the wall!

Follow Through!

Most teams identify possible tasks throughout the course of their meetings. It's always a good idea to have a flipchart ready to record the idea and volunteers for that task. At the end of the meeting, review the "action plan." Make sure the team thoroughly understands the task assigned and the scope of the work. You may even discover that a task doesn't need to be done at all!

Take Names. Make sure you write down the name of at least one person responsible for completing each task. That person is accountable to the team for ensuring the task is completed. It doesn't mean he or she has to do all the work, but he should be responsible for marshalling the right people and resources to get the job done.

Ask the person responsible if they are going to need some help, then quickly identify who will help him. It's a good practice for those people to touch base right after the meeting to set up a time to get together.

Set Specific Due Dates. Rather than "next week," write down February 11. By assigning a specific date, the task becomes much more tangible and can be written on team members' calendars. If appropriate, put the task on a timeline and show how it affects other team events or tasks.

Meeting Minutes. Make sure the action items are captured in the meeting minutes. Typically, minutes are sent out within two days of the meeting. This serves as a quick reminder to each team member.

Follow Up. Then, make sure you devise a system to follow-up on those tasks:

❑ Some teams like to post a "team task list" in a common area. This list has all the assigned, and not yet completed tasks, persons and due dates. As a team member completes a task, the team can check or cross it off the list.

❑ One of the first items on your team's agenda is a report out of the team's "task list." Team members can report out completion, progress, or any delays. Celebrate and congratulate completion. Note progress and see if any help is needed. If there is a delay, don't shoot the messenger! You want to build a work culture that expects assigned tasks to be completed and doesn't hide the facts. Don't assign blame. Instead, allow team members to explain what happened and what they are doing to get the task done. Ask what the team can do to ensure the task is done within a reasonable amount of time.

❑ If it seems like many deadlines are slipping, prioritize your team task list so each team member knows what is vital (it must be done — give it an "A"), important (it should be done — a "B") and nice to have (it could be done — a "C") to your team's work.

❑ Many teams develop ground rules to help each other follow through on tasks. Offer help without being asked. Ask for help — earlier rather than later. Complete all tasks assigned within the agreed upon timeframe.

As you build a system to support the team's follow-through on assigned tasks, the team will start to feel responsible to each other for completing the projects each team member takes on.

Beware of Groupthink

As your team goes about making decisions, it takes just the right combination of courage to speak up and consideration to hear from others. Team decision making is a give-and-take, searching for a win-win.

However, when everything seems to be going swimmingly well — the team is focused on the goal, the team processes are "clicking," decisions are made by consensus — your team may be prone to "groupthink."

Groupthink is a subtle shift from effective decision making to conformity and an unwillingness to "rock the boat." As a result, the team makes low-quality decisions.

Famous examples of groupthink include President Kennedy's Bay of Pigs invasion and the United States government's processing of information from Japan before the Pearl Harbor attack.

Author Jerry Harvey popularized this phenomenon with his story of the "Abilene Paradox." On a hot summer afternoon, someone in his family suggested they drive to Abilene for lunch. Everyone agreed to the idea. As a result, they took a despicably long and hot trip in a car with no air conditioning.

No one had a good time.

When they arrived back home, they discover⌐
no one really wanted to take the trip *but no one* ⌐
to say "no." No one had the courage to challe⌐
idea. Even the person who made the suggestio⌐
want to go!

You are a prime candidate for groupthink ⌐
team:

Is Highly Cohesive. The team works well
together, enjoys each other's company and has
"bonded."

Avoids Different Viewpoints. The team
discounts contrary information and/or discourages
dissent. They may even be insulated from other people
or teams with different viewpoints.

Makes Decisions Easily. Consensus comes
easily — almost too easily. Silence is usually accepted
as consent.

Is Highly Stressed. The team is under high
stress to deliver a quick solution.

Team members can become so concerned about
avoiding conflict that they fail to challenge bad ideas.
To avoid groupthink or the Abilene Paradox, be willing
to challenge ideas, no matter how loyal you feel to the
team. Make sure that no point of view dominates.
Collect information anonymously from team members.
Encourage the role of the devil's advocate. Don't accept
one point of view too readily, and challenge
assumptions.

Present to Management

Your team has worked hard and now needs management support and/or commitment to implement your recommendations. Hopefully, you have been keeping the management group informed of your team's progress, so the presentation should not be "new news." Nevertheless, take time to prepare for your final presentation:

Identify the Audience. Make a list of the names of each of the managers. Next to each of the names, assign a team member to *personally* contact the manager and get a sense for his or her support. If there is a concern, perhaps you can modify the recommendation or address it during the presentation.

Be Clear About Your Team's Goals. What are you trying to do during the presentation: to inform (deliver facts), persuade (shape or change behaviors, attitudes or beliefs) or mobilize (move them to action)? Chances are you are trying to do all three within a limited amount of time. You may find that some of the information-sharing and persuasion can be done in a read-ahead or during the one-on-ones.

Make It Lively. In this multimedia age, keep it moving and dynamic. You can do this by having each

team member take a segment of the presentation. Or use various forms of media: flipcharts, overheads, video or activities. Consider having the presentation on site where the project is, rather than in the typical boardroom.

Keep it Short and Simple. This is not the time to bore them with all the details of your project. Give them the highlights and, if they ask for detail, have it ready. Many teams use the storyboard concept popularized by Walt Disney: Have a simple chart for each major step of the project and conclusions the team made. Then quickly walk the managers through the charts — so they get the flow and feel of the project.

Don't Forget to Ask. I am amazed at how many teams don't ask for what they want. They might even ask for what they *think* management will give them. Be bold. Be specific about what you want: their approval, money, time, people, even their presence!

Tie It to the Business. Make sure there is a clear link between your recommendations and the business strategy or bottom line. List the benefits as well as the costs to the business, both directly and indirectly. Show how the benefits far outweigh the costs and within what time period management should start seeing the benefits for their investment.

Practice. Do a dry-run or walk-through of the presentation. If possible, have another person watch the walk-through and give your team some feedback. Make adjustments as necessary.

Be Flexible. Yes, you have put a lot of time and practice into the presentation, but be flexible and adapt to your audience's needs. Don't get ruffled if they ask a lot of questions! It means they are interested and are evaluating your recommendations — which is precisely what you want them to do. Also, don't be disappointed if they don't give you an answer right then and there. Just make sure you get a firm date as to when they will get back to you.

Chapter Five

Work Together As A Team

It sounds so simple.   Put a bunch of people together, give them a task to do and let them do it. But teams are complex organisms which must balance results with an effective and efficient process while not killing each other along the way!

This chapter focuses on keeping that balance.

EXTRAORDINARY
RESULTS

COOPERATIVE
RELATIONSHIPS

SMOOTH
PROCESS

When people come together to form a team, they go through a predictable pattern of behavior to achieve the work or activity:

Forming	Storming	Norming	Performing
Excited	Defensive	Friendly	Willing
Anxious	Competitive	Sharing	Committed
Proud	Combative	Cohesive	Insightful
Suspicious	Tense	Confident	Satisfied
Fearful Polite	Crunched for time	Willing to provide feedback	Value others' strengths & weaknesses
Reluctant	Resistant to tasks	Comfortable with team ground rules	Attached Delivering

Where the Team is concerned with:

Inclusion	Control	Affiliation	Synergy & Action

Where the Team:

Accepts	Trusts	Cooperates	Performs

Stages of Team Growth

Just as an infant grows into an adult, teams develop and mature into high-performing work teams. Bruce Tuckman described a predictable pattern of development:

Forming. The team members are just coming together, checking each other out and looking for answers. Team members want to know, "What's expected of me? How do I fit in? What are the rules?" Most of the time, the members won't know each other, so they tend to be polite and obedient. You can help get the team through the forming phase by developing or clarifying the team's mission or goal, ground rules, and decision-making methods.

Storming. Their polite enthusiasm quickly gives way to anxiety, frustration and anger. Members openly challenge the mission, the leader and each other, impatient with the lack of progress and approach. They bicker, become defensive, take "sides" and argue even with those they agree with! Don't worry. This is natural and necessary because what emerges from this struggle is a team that is greater than the sum of the individual parts.

Some teams never go through the storming stage because they are fearful that conflict will tear the team apart. But if they fail to go through this stage, they will never learn to deal with their differences. They will remain divided, antagonistic, or will passively resist the team's work.

While storming is the most difficult stage to get through, you can help by allowing each individual to voice an opinion, work through the issues and help the team come to agreement on its next steps.

Norming. As the team emerges from the storm, they learn how to deal with each other. They establish guidelines or "norms" to resolve conflict, make decisions, complete assignments, share leadership and communicate with each other.

In this norming stage, team members find standard ways to do routine things. They drop the hidden agendas, and everyone makes a conscious effort to contribute to the team's work. You might even see some laughing and team comraderie! The main danger in this stage is that the team will avoid conflict rather than disrupt the harmony of the team. You can help the team by testing and modifying the ground rules as necessary and sharing more responsibility and authority among the team members.

Performing. Now the team is ready to move to the performing stage — where the team is mature, focused and working on its mission. Everyone contributes, offers help without being asked, and the team hums like a fine-tuned machine.

Some teams move through the four stages quickly, and some will spend more time in one phase than another. The team can also slip back into a stormy period at any time, particularly if the team has lost its trust or support. The team can even return to the forming stage if it adds or loses a member. As your team makes this journey, look at which stage you are in and how you might help the team move toward the next stage with specific, positive actions.

Build Trust

Trust is a critical component to effective teamwork. The very nature of teams begs each individual team member to trust each other to accomplish the team's task. Team members must be able to rely on and respect each other.

Trust is not bestowed on people; individuals must earn the team's trust. Trust is developed over time as the relationships between team members continue to strengthen. Unfortunately, trust can be betrayed when agreements are broken. Keep the following in mind as you build trust within your team:

Be Honest. Be truthful. Don't play games. If you don't know, aren't sure, or can't say, just tell the team the truth.

Have Integrity. Do what you say you will do. Your teammates are depending on you, so follow through on your commitments. Don't make a promise you can't keep. And if you can't keep the promise, let the team know as soon as humanly possible.

Be Consistent in what you say and do. Be dependable all of the time, not just some of the time.

Share Information. Knowledge is power, and shared knowledge makes the collective team powerful. No one likes to be a mushroom, so don't keep your teammates in the dark.

Manage Conflicts. Rather than avoid conflict, take the time and consideration to work through conflicts and maintain the relationships with your teammates.

Avoid the Five Deadly Sins to Teamwork: talking *at* rather than with your team members, talking *about* other people, talking *around* them, whining and avoiding them altogether!

Accept Inevitable Mistakes. No one is perfect. Everyone makes a mistake (or two). Recognize that each person is doing their best and accept the inevitable mistake. Offer support, encouragement, and help the next time.

Trust is a two-way street. The best way to earn trust from others is to trust them first!

Five Deadly Sins

Ideally, you want to work *with* your team members to accomplish great things. When working *with* your teammates, there is a terrific exchange of ideas and solutions, based on mutual respect and understanding. When working with others, both sides are working together to achieve team success. But sometimes we fall into one of the five sins that undermine our team work:

Talking *At*, Rather Than *With* Others. Much like a parent talks at a child, some may talk at their teammates in an authoritative "I know this, and you don't" tone. People with perceived power typically talk at others in a direct and abrasive manner. They tell them what they know. They aren't really listening to what others' opinions are. They think they are better than others.

In a team environment, that attitude is the kiss of death. In a team, every person has a valid perspective and contribution to make. No one person is better than another.

Talking *About* Other People. Much like when we were kids, when we don't get our way, we talk about other people behind their backs. Talking about someone without that person's ability to share his or her perspective is rude. To the extreme, it is called backstabbing.

When you find yourself talking about another, simply stop! Go find that person and have a meaningful conversation about the circumstances and why you feel the way you do.

Talking *Around* Them. In the era of e-mail and voice-mail, it's easy to flip indirect barbs about our teammates. After all, we are just trying to communicate in the easiest, fastest, and most informal way possible. Sticks and stones may break your bones, but words leave a lasting impression. Especially if you can read or listen to the message over and over again.

If you have a problem, go talk with the person directly. E-mail and voice mail are a great way to share information, not a great technique to solve team problems.

Whining. If you look hard enough, you can always find something to complain about. Constant complainers whine about what happened, didn't happen, what they did, what they didn't do, who they did it with...and the list goes on. Misery loves company. Ever notice how all the complainers band together? Watch out! You can get sucked into the melodrama of how everything is wrong in the world.

What to do? Snap out of it. Stop the complaining. Quit cold turkey. All it does is pull the team down with you.

Avoidance. Rather than deal with the issue or problem, we may choose to ignore it, hoping that it will go away. Rarely, if ever, do team issues go away. They just get worse. By avoiding them, you are doing the team a disservice.

The best thing to do is to have the courage and compassion to give some honest and timely feedback.

Stay Focused

Many teams have a hard time keeping their meetings on track. Regardless of the team's size, type or task, every team can stray off course. To stay focused:

Have an Agenda. If you can, prepare and distribute an agenda ahead of time. An agenda typically has a purpose statement (to share information, make a decision, solve a problem, etc.) and the desired outcomes (greater understanding, a decision, agree on a solution, etc.). An agenda also has a list of topics to be discussed, some estimated time limits for each topic, and the name of the person who will lead the team through the discussion of each topic.

Many small work groups hesitate to be so formal when they have a meeting, but that doesn't mean you can't have an agenda. When the meeting starts, the first agenda item is to build an agenda! Ask everyone if they have a topic that needs to be discussed, agree on how long it should take and who will lead the team through the discussion. Capture the topics, time and leader on a flip chart.

After all ideas have been presented, prioritize the list. Many teams simply number the topics with one as the most important, two the second most important, etc.

Building an agenda "from scratch" (see Chapter Two) shouldn't take any longer than five minutes, and is certainly one of the best prevention strategies you have to keep your team on track. Simply refer to your agenda and go through the topics, starting with number 1, then number 2 and so on.

Have a Timekeeper. Ask a team member to play the role of "timekeeper" to alert the team when they are close to their agreed-upon time limit and to call time.

If you need more time, renegotiate with the team or schedule a separate meeting to discuss the item in more depth. Beware: If you have to keep renegotiating, you aren't being realistic in setting your time limits!

Use a Facilitator. The facilitator's primary job is to keep the team on track. Rather than focusing on content, the facilitator is guiding the process to ensure the team achieves its desired results.

Use a Parking Lot. Post a sheet of flip chart paper on the wall with the headline "Parking Lot." (I like to draw a car to illustrate the point). Capture valuable ideas, thoughts or comments that don't relate to the current topic on the Parking Lot. Then redirect the conversation back to the agenda. The key to using a parking lot is that you always "clear" the items at the end of the meeting.

Record Key Points. Ask another team member to record action items and agreements. As the team makes an agreement or specific people take responsibility for specific tasks, the "recorder" notes the items on a flipchart. Then at the end of the meeting, you can summarize quickly by going through the list!

Keep a Team Memory

Teams share information using "team memory." Team memory is an up-to-date file on all the agendas, minutes, action plans, papers, correspondence and other records that document the team's activities. Keeping a team memory is useful to:

Catch Up. Team membership may change, and the "team memory" allows for new members to catch up.

Retrace Steps. The team may have to retrace its steps to track down problems or errors. Good records make this easier.

Remember Decisions. Some team members may not remember what was decided at an earlier meeting. An up-to-date team memory allows for a quick check.

Prepare to Present. The team may have to prepare a presentation, and team memory makes this much easier.

Typically, the recorder keeps the team memory in a well organized notebook and brings it to each team session.

As a team member, I always take the team agenda (what we planned to do) and capture the "minutes" on the back side of the paper (see next page). I keep this one pager (agenda/minutes) in my daily planner or on file in my team folder. Although not the definitive source like the team memory, my file serves as a nice reminder of where we've been and where we need to go.

Sample Minutes

Date _____ Location _____
Title _____
Purpose _____
Desired Results _____

Brief Summary of topics, decisions or conclusions

Futures File *(items for future consideration but not the next meeting)*

Meeting Critique

+	Δ

Next Meeting Date/Time/Location
Agenda Items:

Speak with Clarity

We all know people who talk a lot...but say nothing. In a team setting, we roll our eyes as soon as the "talker" opens his or her mouth. We brace ourselves for their words — just hoping they will get to the point sooner rather than later.

To be an effective team player, be aware of the message you are trying to send as you speak clearly to your fellow team members.

Try these techniques to enhance your team speaking skills:

Think First. Before you subject others to your rambling thoughts, know what your own attitudes, ideas and feelings are. Then offer your unique perspectives as they add to the team's mission or goal. Speak for yourself. Don't exaggerate with grandiose pronouncements such as "he said..." "she said..." "everyone thinks...."

Say What You Mean. Don't beat around the bush. Be direct, clear and specific. Don't mumble, ramble or speak so softly that others must strain to hear you. Otherwise, your team members will tune out and fill in the blanks for you.

Know Your Team Members. Balance your directness with a dose of sensitivity to how team members may react to what you say. Your goal is to express yourself so team members are able and willing to hear you.

Use Time Wisely. As the numbers in your team increase, the "airtime" becomes much more precious. Be brief and succinct. Make one point at a time. Avoid giving multiple reactions to someone else's comment. If you do need to make several points, number them. Watch for cues that tell you the team is starting to tune you out.

Be Congruent. Make sure your comments, tone and body language match the feeling behind what you are trying to say. Watch your own non-verbal signals for "mixed messages" (such as negative facial expressions) while supporting someone else's idea.

Be Additive. Speak when your contribution is relevant rather than a rehash of what someone else already said.

Ask for Feedback. As you are speaking, watch for subtle clues that the team is listening and understands what you are saying. If you don't get some kind of response (verbal or non-verbal), ask for feedback to ensure you were understood.

Recognize the Inevitable. We have been talking since we were just a few years old, so you would think we would be speaking experts. Wrong! So often we hear "you just don't understand," and "you're not listening," as if the responsibility for effective communication rests with the listener. Accept the inevitability of a communication error. When both speakers and listeners accept responsibility for their errors, they are in the position to strengthen communication and teamwork.

Actively Listen

In his best-selling book, *The Seven Habits of Highly Effective People,* Stephen Covey encourages his readers to "seek first to understand, then to be understood." This habit is just as important for effective teamwork and communication.

Much of the conflict and tension in teams starts with a failure to understand another team member's position, issues or concerns. Try these techniques to actively listen to your teammates:

Prepare to Listen. Shift your focus and attention to the person speaking. Send a non-verbal signal (like turning your head toward the speaker) that you are giving that person your undivided attention.

Actively Listen. Listen with the intent to understand the speaker's words, putting aside your own agenda and immediate response.

Listen for Meaning. Use all your senses to take in information. Listen not only with your ears, but with your eyes and heart. Take in the non-verbals, the tone, the pace, and *feel* what the other person is saying.

Interpret the Message. As we take in all this information focus on understanding what the speaker intends. Put yourself in his or her position. Be aware of your own values and beliefs that act as filters between the speaker's message and your interpretation.

Check for Understanding. Paraphrase or rephrase what was said and check for agreement:

❑ "What I hear you saying is..."

❑ "As I understand it..."

❑ "Let me see if I understand what you are saying..."

❑ "So you think (hope, feel, believe)..."

Caution: Do not parrot word for word what was said. You want to demonstrate that you not only heard what was said, but you understand the meaning behind what was said.

Draw Them Out. Ask open-ended questions to get more information:

❑ "What are your ideas about..."

❑ "What do you think about..."

❑ "Would you please say some more about..."

❑ "Help me to understand..."

❑ "How do you see that working?"

Clarify as Necessary. Ask questions to gain a clearer understanding of what has been said, especially when you think there are differences in the way a word is used or defined:

❑ "What do you mean by..."

❑ "When you say..."

Test the Unsaid. Sometimes, the real issue has not been spoken. If you sense there is something that hasn't been said, test it out:

❑ "I am wondering if you might be concerned about...."

❑ "If we do this, are you concerned about...?"

Reflect the Feeling. This is the key to empathetic listening where you seek to understand the speaker's feeling as well as the words:

❑ "I sense you are ..."

❑ "You look troubled (worried, frustrated)..."

Resist the temptation to advise, criticize or judge when listening and asking questions. Make a conscious effort to understand other points of view. Be sincere and genuine in your desire and you will enhance your teamwork.

Observe the Unspoken

I remember reading a very popular book about body language in the 1970s. If you crossed your arms in front, it meant you were being defensive. If you crossed your legs toward a person, it meant you were open and receptive to their ideas. And the list goes on. The idea was simple. "Read" common gestures and "interpret" them.

Kinesics, the science of non-verbal communication, has evolved beyond "you do this, it means that." Body language complements our spoken language and provides the depth and feeling behind the words, both on a conscious and sub-conscious level. We act out our state of being with a wink of the eye for intimacy, the lift of the eyebrow for disbelief, a nod of the head to show agreement, a shrug of the shoulder for indifference, etc.

You can enhance your team communication through your body language with these simple keys for success:

Consistency. What you say should be consistent with how you say it. You signal your intentions through your facial expressions, eye contact, physical touch, stance, posture, movement, gestures and closeness to the other person. We have all experienced the incongruency of someone saying "yes," but shaking their head side to side, signaling "no." It makes us confused and we are not sure what to believe — the yes, no or something in between.

Awareness. Just as you are conscious of the words you are saying, be aware of what your body is saying. We typically don't even notice the non-verbal messages we continually send to our fellow team members. As you become more conscious of your body language, your words and actions will become more congruent.

Context.   Examine what is going on in the environment around you.   If your teammate has crossed her arms in front, it might be that she is cold, not defensive.   A teammate rubbing his eyes might mean that he is tired, or he just got a new pair of glasses! We typically try to "read between the lines" and make assumptions based on our own reactions and history (or what we read in some book).   Test your assumptions before you leap to conclusions.

Try starting out your team meetings with a quick "check-in" — a word, phrase or statement which allows team members to say what's on their minds.   It provides an opportunity to share with the team whatever might be keeping them from fully participating in the discussion. A check-in allows each team member to voice professional or personal issues which may be affecting team communication.

Variation.   Everyone has a unique and predicatable pattern of non-verbal communication: the way they sit, hold their arms and listen to people. Watch for changes in others' body language — a shift in posture, a sudden movement, an arm outstretched. Ask yourself: "What is causing this shift?" It may be a good indicator of readiness — to talk, to agree, to object, to intervene.   It also may be that the person is tired of sitting and wants to stretch! Take advantage of these shifts and draw that person into the team's work.

Feedback: The Breakfast of Champions

The single most important skill in solving team problems is the ability to give and receive constructive feedback. When a problem arises, most people tend to get defensive, react negatively and then justify their actions. Others simply sit on their feelings for the sake of team harmony and hope the situation will take care of itself.

When a problem arises, team members must take the responsibility to give feedback to each other in a meaningful way, as well as to listen to the feedback as an opportunity for growth and improvement. Feedback is often called the "breakfast of champions" in that high performers *ask* for feedback specifically for the purpose of improving their performance, processes and relationships.

Whether giving praise or constructive criticism, try these proven methods for effectively giving feedback:

Be Timely. Give your feedback as close as possible to the time the behavior is demonstrated. Be sensitive to giving feedback in front of others — consider waiting until you can say something in private.

Ask if It is Wanted. Feedback is best delivered when the other person is in a position to listen to you. Your purpose should be to help the person improve. Don't put the person on the spot (gotcha!) or show the team how smart you are.

Phrase as a Statement, not a question. Questions suggest that the person must do something about your feedback. Try not to make "right" or "wrong" judgements on the behavior. Don't second-guess why the person did what they did. Simply state the observed behavior and use "I" statements to allow the person to see what effect the behavior had on you.

Be Descriptive. Tell the person what you saw him or her do or say. Give specific examples. Provide enough detail so that the behavior is well understood *and* can be acted upon. Address only those behaviors that the person has the ability to change.

Don't Exaggerate. Words such as "always, never, everybody, nobody" leave lots of room for argument. Talk about things you know for certain. Base your feedback on facts, not on speculation or opinion.

Be Positive, Honest and Direct. Don't beat around the bush. Speak from the heart. Help the person hear and accept your compliments. Remember: You give feedback because you are concerned about the other person. We usually don't even waste our time or breath on people we don't care about.

When receiving feedback:

Actively Listen. Don't become defensive or argumentative. Ask for specific examples or questions to clarify. Understand what the speaker is saying and why that person is taking the time to give you feedback. Acknowledge the other person's point of view.

Think About It. Acknowledge the valid points and, if appropriate, change your behavior.

Say Thank You. Respect the person for taking the time to speak with you. Sometimes it is more painful to bring up the issue than it is to resolve it.

Ask for Help to Improve. Many times, we aren't even aware of how our behavior impacts the team dynamic. Agree on steps forward and ask your fellow team members to gently remind you when you fall into the same problem.

You can also use these methods to tell other team members when they have done something well. As your team becomes more comfortable with giving and receiving feedback, the team's work will move toward higher levels of performance.

Influence Others

Influence is a complex set of behaviors and interactions to get the results you want from someone else. There are many ways to influence others — and most team members try to convince others of what they want and then sell the benefits. If this works, great! If not, you may want to try some other techniques:

Identify your Purpose or what your team is looking for. Is it to accomplish something? Influence someone to make a commitment? Take responsibility for something? Get important information?

Consider the Context or what is going on with the organization or individual. Evaluate what has happened in the past and your current relationship. How will this help or hinder your ability to influence?

Select a Strategy which will help you achieve results as well as further your relationship. Here are several approaches with possible "sentence starters":

Ask Open-Ended Questions in a way that doesn't imply either a right answer or assume responsibility. "What do you think about..." "How might we do this?" "What are your ideas about...."

Ask for Clarification to gain a clearer understanding of what has been said. "What do you mean by...." "When you say...."

Build On What Has Been Said to deepen or extend the thinking. "You mentioned...could you say more about that?" Or try "Help us to understand...." "How do you see that working?"

Check for Understanding. Paraphrase or rephrase what was said and ask for agreement or correction. "What I hear you saying is...." "As I understand it...." "Let me see if I understand what you are saying...." "So you think (hope, feel, believe)...."

Identify with the Other's Situation, experience or feelings and how those things could be affecting the other person. "If I were you, I might be feeling...." "I remember how I felt when...."

Paint a Picture. Describe the future in today's terms, helping the other person to envision the results. "I can see us..." "Picture this...."

Generate Enthusiasm by urging the other person to join the team in taking action. "I know we can..." "I believe as a team...."

Offer Incentives or negotiate a fair exchange. "If you do this, we will...." "In exchange, we will...."

Test the Unsaid. Sometimes the real issue has not been spoken. If you sense there is something which hasn't been said, test it out: "I am wondering if you might be concerned about...." "If we do this, are you concerned about...?"

Ask a Show Stopper question: "What would it take for you to...." or "What could we do so you would agree?"

If you still cannot influence the situation, you can simply walk away and come back another time.

Energize Your Team's Creativity

Teams are terrific for creating new ideas. A well-run creative session journeys into unchartered waters, so it's important to build a safe harbor for creative ideas to flourish. Unleash your team's creative juices with the following ground rules:

Everyone Is Creative. Don't accept the excuse, "I'm not creative." By getting up each day, everyone "creates" their day, so we are all creative in some fashion. You just haven't had the right opportunity to discover your hidden talent!

What's Said Here, Stays Here. In his book, *Rousing Creativity*, Floyd Hurt asserts that confidentiality counts. "If word spreads that ol' Joe said something dumb, not only will ol' Joe not come back, but neither will anyone else." For a free expression of ideas, nothing leaves the room unless everyone agrees.

Move! Movement inspires creativity. Stand up, move around, wave your arms, draw pictures, etc.

Be Spontaneous. Don't worry about what others will think of your idea. Don't think too long or too hard. Just let the creative energy of the group unlock your traditional thinking. Some of the best ideas have come from quiet team members who never considered themselves to be "creative." But when they allowed themselves to speak spontaneously, their contributions were huge!

Consider Every Idea. Respond to every idea with interest and curiosity, instead of criticism. Look for the positive aspects of the idea. If you need a jump start, try "this idea could work if...." Negative aspects simply become hurdles to overcome. Rather than saying "that won't fit," try asking "how can we make it bigger?"

Pitch In. When a team member can't fully express his or her idea, assist in developing the idea by asking questions and making suggestions.

Hitchhike On Others' Ideas. When someone says something that sparks a new idea, acknowledge the original idea. Then build on it. Everyone likes a little recognition and it builds the team's spirit as well.

Check Your Bearings. Especially in creative sessions, it's easy to wander off course. Be sure to check your bearings frequently (are you really trying to solve the problem?) to make sure you are still moving ahead on the topic.

Allow For "Soak Time." People often need time alone to create and consider new ideas. Set aside some time for the ideas to "soak" before any decision is made.

Be Patient. Creative sessions start out lively and chaotic. As the team begins to focus, capture key elements on a flipchart pad and refine using a team consensus process.

Be Aware of Strategic Moments

Strategic moments are those key times when the group is faced with a variety of possible ways to proceed. By choosing one particular direction, the team is making a commitment that is not easily reversed.

You can tell a strategic moment when the team begs the question, "What do we do now?" Usually, the answer is a key conclusion, realization, insight, group decision or other significant event.

Strategic moments are both a crisis and an opportunity. The crisis is one of faith. Can the team really agree on a path forward? If we choose a particular path, can we be successful?

The opportunity exists for the team to strike out boldly, declare its decision and work together to achieve success.

When facing a strategic moment:

Call It.   Recognize that the team is facing a strategic moment where the selection of an appropriate course of action will be critical to the team's success. Make sure everyone understands the importance of the moment.

Make a Conscious Choice.   The team is in a quandary. What to do? Whatever you decide, make an intentional choice.   If left undecided, a trivial strategic moment can become a problem in the future.

Aim for Consensus.   Since this is a key decision, aim for consensus so that all team members can live with *and* support the decision upon implementation.

Critique Your Team's Work

At the close of each meeting, conduct a quick, short critique. On a flipchart or whiteboard, draw a line down the middle to make two columns. At the top of the left column, write a plus sign "+" and a delta sign "Δ" on the right column.

+	Δ

What Went Well? Ask the team to think about what went well. List members' answers under the "plus" column. Teams typically comment on their progress, team participation, process used or meeting logistics. When all ideas are exhausted, thank the group for the positive feedback. Encourage the team to keep up the good work!

Done Differently? Next, look to the "deltas" or things the team would have done differently. Notice the phrasing; it is much more positive and upbeat than asking the team to identify the negatives or "what we did wrong." List the deltas without commenting on them. You may have to be patient.... Many team members may be uncomfortable giving team feedback initially, but, when they recognize the value of the critique, will open up.

Preventions. Wait for all the deltas to go up on the board, and *then* ask the team what they can do to prevent the deltas from happening again. Some items might be one-time occurrences, and the team will agree that nothing needs to be done. Other items may require action from the team. Agree on what that action is, who will do it, and by when.

For example, "fewer side conversations" was recorded as a "do differently." Ask, "What might we do to prevent side conversations at our next session?" There will be a flurry of responses, and the team will settle down to a quick, simple solution such as add "no side conversations" to the ground rules.

Thank 'Em! Quickly thank the team for taking the time to critique its teamwork, reinforcing the strengths and taking action on areas for improvement. Ask for any final comments and adjourn the meeting.

For Team Leaders: If you are leading the team, don't be defensive during the critique. Avoid attempting to explain why you did what you did, but feel free to ask questions for clarification or for specifics. After the meeting, take a few minutes to conduct your own personal critique (have your co-leader or facilitator join you).

Ask: Did we achieve our intended results? Did we use or follow an effective process? Did we work well together? Overall, what worked well and what could we have done differently?

Compare your impressions with the team's critique. Look for patterns or trends. One contrary comment certainly should be considered, but if there were several contrary comments (regardless of the reasoning), take a closer look.

Based on the critiques, identify one skill, behavior, tool or technique you think could enhance the quality of the team's work. Develop a personal action plan as well as a measure of your success. After all, you want to know whether your actions improved your teamwork!

Team Measurements

You should be measuring your team on three levels:

❑ **Team Performance**. Are the team's products meeting their key stakeholders' expectations? (e.g. increase sales, reduce customer complaints, reduce cycle time).

❑ **Team Process.** Is the team becoming more competent at its work? (e.g. making decisions, holding meetings, creating outputs, effecting change). Is the team "healthy" as defined by the team and the organization?

❑ **Individual Growth.** Are the individual team members contributing, learning and growing as they are serving on the team?

For each of these three areas, agree on the team's goals and a vital few measures to track progress. These measures must be easily quantified (numbers of or percentage of) and can be:

❑ Objective (e.g. financial, cycle time).

❑ Subjective (e.g. behavioral or observable).

Once the team knows *what* to measure, agree on *who* is going to measure, *how* they will measure, and *how often* they will measure it. Don't forget to use technology to your advantage!

Set up an easy way to communicate progress such as a trend chart. The horizontal or x-axis is time (daily, weekly, monthly, quarterly) and the vertical or y-axis is the unit of measure (performance, process or growth).

On the trend chart, plot four points:

❑ Establish a baseline (where we are now).

❑ The goal (where we want to be).

❑ Whether the measure should be increasing or decreasing (I like to use a thumb up or down).

❑ The "benchmark" or how the best-in-class performs, if known.

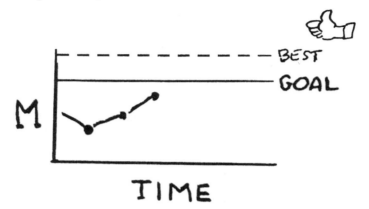

Keep these charts visible for all team members to see. Review your goals and metrics often. What seemed reasonable yesterday may not resonate in today's changing marketplace.

The best team metrics support the overall organizational mission and vision. They reflect the team's added value. Key stakeholders and team members are involved in the process. The team has control over what is measured and how it is measured. The metrics are viewed as a vehicle for continuous improvement.

Assess Team Effectiveness

First, let's start with a simple definition of team effectiveness. The team:

❑ Attains its goal(s)

❑ Uses an effective and efficient process

❑ Enjoys working together.

All three conditions are necessary for effective teamwork. If the team gets along and fails to achieve its objective, or if the team accomplishes the goal, but members end up despising each other, the team has not been as effective as possible.

There are lots and lots of formal and informal team assessment tools that you can purchase "off the shelf." In the event you decide to use one of these instruments, follow these steps to maximize the experience:

Know Why. It seems obvious, but why are you assessing the team's work? Team assessments are meant to be used as constructive feedback to the team to reinforce what is working well and to provide insight on areas for improvement. It should not be used as a performance management tool.

Know What is Important. Clarify the behaviors valued by the organization *and* the team. You may find a difference between what they currently value and what they *should* value. This discussion can get really interesting. In the meantime, you will validate why the organization thinks teamwork is important.

Select an Instrument, based on importance, ease of use, type of data generated, and cost. Or, if you are adventurous, cobble your own assessment taking from the "best of the best."

Keep in mind that questionnaires are the most common sources of information. They keep the measurement process relatively objective and produce quantifiable and repeatable data.

Prepare. Consider how the assessment will be distributed, how it will be returned, how to guard against breach of anonymity, and who will process the information. There are several software programs that will allow you to do these types of assessments on-line and will compile and summarize the data. Be sensitive to how the team will receive the news that they are going to be assessed. It could be perceived negatively.

Complete the Assessment. Give the team members the instrument as well as a written cover letter that includes why the assessment is being done, instructions, the deadline for returning the assessment, and a meeting date to present the results and next steps.

Collect and Summarize the Data. Have more than one member of the team involved; otherwise, others might feel the collector (especially if it is the team leader) could misinterpret or misuse the data. Organize the information into a format that presents the results concisely and visually.

Interpret the Data. Have the team meet to agree on the team's strengths and opportunities for improvement. Spend some time savoring and celebrating the team's strengths. Then objectively look at how the team can get even better.

Create a Plan. Develop a plan to improve the team's work with specific action items including who is going to do what and by when. Agree on how the team will follow up on its commitments.

Identify Next Steps. Consider the first assessment to be a "baseline" of the team's work. Agree to check the team's progress periodically to see if the team is becoming more effective. Agree on how often the team will be assessed. Set a goal for where you would like to see the team next time!

Reward Team Efforts

Most American companies and organizations reward individual performance. We celebrate our individuality and want to be compensated and rewarded for our efforts. However, if you want your people to perform as a team, you must reward them as a team.

What Gets Measured Gets Done. Bolt your reward system to your company and team's metrics. Make sure your team has defined goals and measures of success. Reward results, not just activity.

Compensate the Team. Once a team-oriented infrastructure is in place (goals, measures, appraisal systems, training), then your compensation system (salary increases, promotions, and bonuses) can be tied to actual team performance. The possibilities range from a system where all team members share equally in the rewards to a peer evaluation system to reward team and individual contributions.

Share the Wealth. In some instances, teams are highly dependent on other teams, functions or other companies! Consider a profit-sharing or stock option plan that distributes the rewards among all of the teams, based on the performance of the higher-level unit to which they contribute.

Pay for Skills. Compensate team members based on the skills they have rather than the jobs they hold. Skill-based pay systems motivate team members to learn new skills (e.g. cross training, self-management, information technology, business skills) that benefit the team, increasing its potential for high performance. The key is to encourage team learning, not just ticket-punching.

It's a Matter of Time. As people experience working together on teams, they will become more comfortable with their team skills, relationships and abilities to succeed as a team. As the numbers of teams succeed, the organization will begin to recognize that teams are a powerful strategy for achieving specific business results. Over time, this teeming critical mass will push up against the current reward system in support of tying their rewards to the performance of others *in addition to* their own performance. Just make sure the two systems aren't working at cross purposes!

Be Patient. People's pay is an emotional issue. It will take time before team members and leaders are ready to accept a literal shift in values to support collaborative decision making, collective goals, team performance, and shared rewards.

Recognize Good Team Performance

A team is a group of individuals...and you must recognize each person's contributions to the team's overall success. While money is a powerful motivator, there are things you can do, large and small, that can recognize team members who are  overworked, serving multiple masters, logging miles to attend critical meetings and doing whatever else it takes to be successful.

Visibility. Provide opportunities for team members to be visible within the organization (e.g. presenting papers, project results, management briefings). Include members' names on team deliverables such as reports or presentations.

Ongoing Development. Provide developmental opportunities to team members, such as training programs and special assignments. Support their involvement in industry or professional conferences. Encourage them to visit other companies to share the learnings and results of their work. Provide reasonable time off and/or pay tuition for degree or certification programs.

Environment. Provide state of the art and/or comfortable equipment and flexible working conditions.

Team Photos. Take team photographs. Post them on the bulletin board or publish them in the company newsletter or industry and trade journals.

Thank You Notes. In this age of electronics, an unexpected personal thank you note works wonders.

At the minimum, write a formal letter to every team member at the conclusion of the project.

Small Gifts. Send flowers, a gift basket, tickets to a movie or some small token to team members who have been working long hours, traveling excessively, or who you have caught doing something right.

Celebrate. Pizza party, pool party, BBQ, bowling, or the U-Name-It event at the completion of the project as well as important milestones along the way. Here are some ideas:

❑ Bring in a bottle of non-alcoholic champagne and glasses (plastic will do, but it's a lot more fun with glass!). Start the toast with "I am thankful this team is....." Clink glasses, take a sip and encourage others to continue the toast!

❑ Have each team member share his or her most memorable team moment.

❑ Have a potluck lunch. Encourage team members to stay and mingle rather than run back to the office.

❑ Have team members share what they think is the team's most significant accomplishment and what contributed to its success.

❑ Share what each individual does to celebrate success (such as go out to dinner) and then agree on how the team will celebrate its success.

❑ Bring in a Polaroid camera and take team pictures.

❑ Have all the team members sit in a circle. Take a big ball of yarn and wrap one end around your finger. Throw the ball to another team member and thank that person for a specific contribution or accomplishment. That team member then wraps a bit of yarn around his or her finger and continues the process. You can even send it back to the same person! Watch the interconnected web the team weaves....

❑ Go for brisk team walk in the afternoon cool air and return to a mug of simmering hot apple cider.

❑ Share what you gained from working on the team and what are you thankful for learning.

Your best opportunity to recognize individual contributions and relationships is at the beginning of each team meeting. As you start, draw attention to roles and functions and the intended relationships between them. Some ideas to consider:

You're Special. Send the signal that each team member is special and has a valuable position on the team. Provide a copy of the agenda in a special folder with team member names. Prepare name tents bearing names and team roles. Ask members to stand and introduce themselves.

Hear Ye. Hear Ye. As team members introduce themselves, ask them to share their roles, functions, team stories or other noteworthy contributions.

Check In. Ask team members if anyone has anything of interest to share or to recognize other team members for their contributions since the last time you met.

Team Activities. Icebreakers are great ways to jump-start a meeting. They are lively, fun and interactive. Share the role of leading the team through a new icebreaker. Have fun with the activity and with the leader. At the conclusion, don't forget to thank team members for setting a positive tone for the rest of the meeting. By allowing a different team member to lead the team activity, they are visibly contributing to the team.

Tap Into Their WIIFM. Each person comes to the team with their own agenda or WIIFM (What's In It For Me). As a group, take the time to answer the question (WIIFM) for each team member. (Hint: With Generation X and Y teams, this form of recognition is a must.)

Pop In. Have the sponsor or champion "pop in" to a team meeting and actually know what the team is doing and how it is contributing to the organization's success. Better yet, brief the champion with specifics about how each team member has contributed to the team's success. Coach the champion to express appreciation for each person's involvement and team success.

Thank 'Em. As you kick off the meeting, remember to thank team members for their contributions since the last time you met. Rather than read a list, weave your compliments into the conversation. When team members offer an idea or suggestion, thank them for their initiative and contribution. The key is to be consistent in your recognition as well as authentic and genuine in your thanks.

Improve Your Own Teamwork

Take a few moments to improve your own teamwork. Take a look at your organization or team's performance standards for being a "good team player" or other similar performance criteria. Look at the situation from your supervisor's and team members' perspective. Read through the criteria and ask yourself: What am I doing well? Acknowledge your strengths (there are some!). Be sure to continue and reinforce what is working well.

Then take a look at what you could do differently. Are there some behaviors you could start doing or do better? If in doubt, ask your teammates for some honest feedback on your team performance. Identify three things that you could do to enhance your team skills. Then build a small action plan to put these ideas in place.

For example, you discover that you don't ask others for their opinions. You decide that you want to start asking others' for their opinions — especially after you offer an opinion. You decide on the following actions:

- ❑ Craft several questions to ask ("what do you think about...").

- ❑ Review action plan before all team meetings.

- ❑ Make a concerted effort to ask for their opinions.

- ❑ Review how you did after the meeting.

Unfortunately, many organizations do not have established performance criteria. If this is the case, you may want to ask your team to agree on what makes a good team member. You may even find some guidelines in the team's ground rules, operating norms, or guiding principles (or consider the ground rules we discussed in chapter two).

Chapter Six

Leverage Teams With Technology

Technology expands our options for ways of working together, sharing information and collaborating as a team.

Unfortunately, most people are introduced to specific technologies because the organization decided to purchase and install it. Team members feel compelled to use it because it is "there" without establishing ground rules for effective use.

Even today, with the prevalence of voice-mail and e-mail, there are few organizations that have a systematic approach to using these terrific technologies. As a result, improper use can inflict tremendous damage to the team's work.

To leverage these technologies appropriately, organizations need to ensure team members have and know how to use compatible equipment, provide organization-wide guidance on appropriate usage, and allow teams to develop their own ground rules for success.

This chapter focuses on the ground rules for appropriate use of the most common technologies teams use.

A Wide Range of Team Technologies

	Face to Face	**Dispersed**
Low	Flipcharts Whiteboards Overheads	Memos Faxes Phone calls Conference calls
	Electronic whiteboards Copyboards	Voice-mail E-mail
	LCD panels Multimedia projectors	Videoconferencing
	Physical team tooms	Virtual team rooms Team bulletin boards Internet/online Broadcasting Dataconferencing tools
High	Groupware Meeting Room Software	LAN meeting room software Internet-based meeting room software

Choose the Appropriate Technology

The more time you spend in team meetings, the more your team will need to leverage technology to make your time together valuable. Some technology tools — such as whiteboards, flipcharts and overhead projectors and have been around for years. Others — including digital whiteboards, multimedia projectors, meeting room software and dataconferencing tools — are surfacing as wonderful opportunities for team communication.

As you evaluate and select from the various technologies which may benefit your team, consider the following factors:

Availability. The technology should be readily available and accessible to everyone involved on the team.

Training. Everyone should have access to adequate training to learn how to use the technology appropriately.

Skills. Either through training, performance support systems or other creative means, everyone should have adequate skills to be competent and comfortable while using the technology.

Time. All team members know and respect the most convenient times to send and receive messages — from across the table as well as across time zones.

Expense. Initially, the technology may appear to be too expensive, but when you factor in the time, personnel, equipment, travel and other costs, you may be surprised to find how reasonable that videoconference system (or the hourly rental rate) really is!

Importance. Important messages, especially those involving feedback, are best communicated face to face, so team members can hear the verbal and nonverbal messages.

Culture. Some cultures, such as the United States, Canada and many northern European nations, tend to value the verbal content of the message. Others, such as Asian and Middle Eastern countries, tend to value face-to-face interactions. Consider the need to hear not only the verbal message, but also the informal interactions, physical exchanges, non-verbal cues, and tone of voice.

Language. For some team members, English is a secondary language. Native speakers should be considerate in using technologies, especially in their speech and written materials.

Ground Rules. Whatever technology your team selects, agree on ground rules or agreements on how to use the technology, when to use it, explicit protocols and formats.

Preference. Lastly, ask your teammates which technology they prefer and might be willing to use, try or experiment! Although technology is drastically changing the way teams work, the technology must match our preferences and work patterns in order to be truly effective.

Bottom Line. Technology is an enabler, not the answer for weak team skills. Use just the right technology to help your team accomplish its mission and goals.

Telephone Conference Calls

Telephone conference calls are a low cost meeting alternative for teams located in different places. They are great for routine status reports and for short-term, problem solving meetings, but not if you follow your instincts to just grab the phone and start talking! Conference calls are not as easy as one-on-one phone conversations, so follow these tips or ground rules for effective conference calls:

Know Your Phone. Whether you are using your office phone, cellular or conference phone, know how to use it, mute it, and connect to others without disconnecting.

Use a Moderator. One person (typically the person who initiated the call) should be the moderator. Start with a "roll call" of attendees and their location so that everyone knows who is on the line and announce when new members join in. Give a short, precise overview of the purpose and goal of the call, followed by a simple, clear agenda. Ask the participants to follow the agenda and conference call ground rules.

Keep Up the Pace. Most participants usually speak very slowly, careful of what they say and how they say it. But the average person is able to decode verbal information four to five times faster than the average speaking rate. This makes for a very long, tedious meeting! The moderator should set the tone of the conference call by speaking at a regular rate with good inflection and intensity. Other participants will then follow the leader in style and rate. The moderator should also ask the participants to limit their contributions to a reasonable length (for example one or one and one-half minutes) and allow questions for clarification.

Manage Voice Traffic. The more people you have on the line, the greater the potential for overload and domination of a few people. Limit the number of people involved in the conference call to team members and one or two scheduled speakers. Ask the participants to state their names and location each time they speak. Recognize that one individual at one location will have more "air time" than several people huddled around a speaker phone at another location. If possible, questions should be directed to specific individuals. For example, "John, will you share your perspective on this issue?" or "Mary, could you please clarify that issue?" The moderator may serve as a "gatekeeper" to ensure everyone has the opportunity to participate.

Take a Poll. At critical moments in the meeting, poll the participants for their input. Call out each name and ask for their opinion, comment or vote. Recognize that this will take time, especially for larger groups, but is worthwhile for critical issues where the team must make a decision to move forward.

Use Handouts. Where possible, mail or fax information to be used during the conference call. Quantifiable data such as sales forecasts, trend charts, and other descriptive data is helpful to have prior to the meeting so that everyone is looking at and commenting on the same information.

Phone conference calls can save time, travel costs, energy and hassle — especially if the team follows these basic ground rules to enhance the effectiveness of your next conference call.

Stay Connected with Electronic Mail

Are you sharing information with all of your team members? Do you routinely pass along important discussions you have had, things you learned, or intelligence you gathered?

If you are like most, you'll tell the people you are close to, or wait until the next meeting before you share your information.

But today's teams can't wait and they are highly dependent on the sharing of information between *all* team members — not just the ones you happen to like or work next to.

As a direct result of improved communications technology, teams are taking advantage of the many quick ways to share information and stay connected — especially through electronic mail (e-mail) and voice-mail.

Set Up a Group List so that you can write or record one message and send it to all team members at once. Be careful, however, if one of your team members or someone who needs to know is not "in the loop."

Agree on the Team Ground Rules on how you are going to use e-mail and voice-mail. Agree on how often you are going to check your mailboxes, how quickly you will respond to your mail, and the format of the standard outgoing voice-mail message. Most teams agree to check their mail at least daily and to respond within one working day.

Send your E-Mail "to" the people who need to take action, and "copy to" (cc) those who only need to know. On the subject line, clearly state the purpose of the message (status of xyz project, my discussion with M. Mouse, new information on abc). Use group lists appropriately; be selective and don't overcopy.

Write Action Items First. If any actions are required, write the specific action, who is required to complete the task, and the date by which it should be completed at the beginning of the message. Then write the detail of the message.

Be Courteous. Please DON'T SHOUT IN CAPITAL LETTERS — it's tough to read! Keep it short and simple. Use bullets instead of prose paragraphs. A good rule of thumb to consider: If it takes you longer than a screen to write, you probably should go see or call the person directly.

Respond Selectively. Add "FYI — no reply needed" if no response is needed. You are not expected to respond to a "FYI" or "copy to/cc" message. Reply only to the sender; be careful of the "Reply to All" default option. No need to send "ok!" or "thanks!"

Think Before You Send. Ensure the information is clear and the tone is correct. E-mails should not be a stream of consciousness or jumble of fragmented thoughts.

Stay Connected with Voice-Mail

When using voice-mail, use the same care and consideration as you do with e-mail. Set up a group list and agree on ground rules.

Think First. Think about what you want to say and note a few important points you want to cover.

Send Your Voice-Mail. When you record your team message, tell them who the message is being sent to (all team members), the purpose of the message, any actions that need to be taken and by when. Then you can go into the detail of the message, making sure you cover the important points. The key is to speak clearly and concisely. Do not babble or repeat yourself.

Access. If you can, always provide the method you can be reached, when you will return to the office, or the ability to access a "live body." Some people just don't like voice-mail, and you need to be aware of their needs — especially if it's a customer!

Call Back. Always return others' voice-mail promptly. If you don't need a response, say so!

When used correctly, e-mail and voice-mail can save you precious team meeting time otherwise spent in bringing everyone up to speed.

LCD Panels and Multimedia Projectors

A simple yet effective way of using technology is to have the recorder or "technographer" capture the ideas on a notebook and project the team's work through a LCD/multimedia projector. This is similar to posting the ideas on a flipchart; however, there are several benefits:

More Detail. You can project more information on a screen than you can write on a flipchart. You can view spreadsheets, project timelines, drawings and other visuals which would otherwise be hard to duplicate.

Easy Changes. You can make changes quickly and easily as long as the technographer is familiar with the equipment and the software.

Quick Computing. Computers do the math much quicker than humans do! When you tally team votes or use a mathematical model, have a "pre-made" spreadsheet ready to input the missing data, then press a button and poof! The results are posted immediately.

Quick Copies. After the team has made its changes, you can quickly make a printed or electronic copy for all to take back to their workplaces.

Impressive Signal. Using multimedia is still new to many teams and sends the signal that the team is important enough to deserve "high-tech" support.

Remember Murphy's Law: What can go wrong will go wrong. So get to the meeting site early, set up, check the equipment and leave the power on.

Videoconferencing

What works well for successful face-to-face meetings is even more important when you use video and audio technology to link people in different locations.

Have a Crisp, Simple Agenda and make sure everyone has access to any important information before the meeting begins.

Arrive Early. Be at your desktop or the videoconferencing room a few minutes early and familiarize yourself with the controls, the monitor and camera placement. Depending on the type of system you are using, identify as the "controller" one person who can adjust your camera position and focus, monitor screens, volume etc.

Check In. Have each person check in with his or her name and location at the beginning of the call. Be patient as other site(s) gets used to their controls! Also, get a sense for inevitable time delays.

Agree on the Basics. Agree on the meeting purpose, agenda and timeframes. Unless you have exclusive control over your system, videoconferences always start and end precisely on time. You can't afford to run overtime...or else the system will shut down!

Agree on Ground Rules to manage the participation. The more locations you have online, the greater the potential for domination by a few people or meeting breakdown. For example, ask the participants to state their names and locations each time they speak. The moderator may serve as a "gatekeeper" to ensure everyone has the opportunity to participate or to manage the airtime when multiple people start talking. When making a key decision, ask for participants to "weigh in" with their opinions.

Out of Sight. Recognize some participants may be connected by phone without the benefits of video — or one-way video where they can see you but you can't see them (or vice versa). Pay particular attention to your ground rules so you don't forget these "out of sight, out of mind" participants!

WISYWG. What you see is *not* what you get. Don't assume the other sites can't see you. Most of the time, their display is wider than what you see. When speaking, look at the camera (not the monitor). You may not be able to pick up on the participants' non-verbals, so pay close attention to what they say and how they say it.

Be Careful What You Say. You are "broadcasting" information which, like a cellular phone, can be intercepted. So don't give away the company secrets!

Collaborative Technology or Groupware

Groupware is software specifically designed to facilitate human interaction and information. Whether all the team members are in the same room, or dispersed around the world, automated meeting tools facilitate the team process.

Have you ever used "collaborative technology" or "electronic meeting support"? Laptop computers are networked to create a "chatroom" to conduct the meeting. Everyone can key comments and ideas into the machines simultaneously. All of the comments appear on everyone's monitor and are projected on a screen in front of the room.

There are some obvious advantages to conducting a meeting through collaborative technologies:

All at Once. Everyone can "talk" at once. Team members can key in their comments at the same time and the computer collects them with lightning speed. Team members don't have to wait for someone else to finish their verbal comment before speaking. Introverts don't have to worry about being shy. Their voice is just as "loud" as the other meeting attendees.

Lightning Fast. In approximately 15 seconds, the groupware program can produce the statistics of a 15 person vote including standard deviation, mean, mode, high, low, Kendall's Coefficient and Z-Value (the deviation of the individual's vote from the mean of the group).

Automatic Team Memory. All the information is keyed into the computers. You don't have carry flipcharts home and desperately try to remember exactly what we meant when the recorder wrote down "mgt rpt req" on the flipchart. All you have to do is click, click and voila! A complete printout of what was said.

Anonymity. When you see a comment on the screen in the front of the room, no one knows who it came from. All they know is that there is a comment on the screen in the front of the room and they have to deal with it. No one has to fear retribution or punishment or exposure unless they choose to reveal that they are the author of that comment.

It's Different

This anonymity creates a completely different atmosphere in the meeting. Attendees can vote the way they really feel without worrying about their boss seeing them raise their hand for the "wrong" option. They can say what they want the way they want and see how their comment is received without having to reveal themselves. Something as seemingly deadly as, "Get focused, John," when keyed in as a message to the Chief Executive Officer, can be totally accepted because of the anonymity.

J.R. Holt, *JRH Associates*

Beware of Hiding Behind Technology

While technologies enable group collaboration across geographical boundaries, some team members will hide behind technology to avoid human interaction.

I have seen two team members fire off e-mails to each other even though they work within fifty feet of each other.

On the other hand, the appropriate use of technology can create great spaces for teams to do great work without having to come together *as often.*

Technology will not replace human contact. Teams will still need to come together eyeball to eyeball to build the trust that is so important to extraordinary teamwork.

As you use technology, recognize new team members may not be as familiar with these gadgets as everyone else. They may be anxious about using new tools. They probably don't know who is responsible to set up and maintain it. And who do they go to with questions?

To ease their worries, orient them to the ground rules to effectively leverage the technology. Answer the "five w's and an h":

Why. Why do I need this technology? Why has the organization invested in this technology? Why should I use it?

Who. Who else uses this technology? Who has the technical expertise in the event I have a question? Who decides if I can use this technology? Who else can access this technology (confidentiality of information)?

What. What do I need to know to use the technology effectively and efficiently? What else does the technology do? What am I *not* supposed to do (or touch)? What are the protocols that should be followed? What format should I follow? What maintenance am I responsible for? What do I do if....

When. When is it appropriate to use this technology? When am I *not* supposed to use this technology? When do I...?

Where. Where do I use the technology? Can I take it elsewhere? Can I access it somewhere else? If so, where else? Where do I...?

How. How do I use this technology? How is this technology going to make my work easier, better, cheaper or faster? How should I maintain this technology? How do I ensure proper use? How do I...?

One Good Idea

Is your team too complacent or too reliant on the conveniences of electronic communication such as faxes, e-mail and telephones?

Agree to put away the "electronic gadgets" for a day. If you need something, get up. Get out. Network. Do lunch. Circulate.

Virtual Teams

Virtual teams work across space, time, and organizational boundaries. Unlike conventional teams, teammates can be in different geographic locations, time zones, departments or among different companies! Reinforced with faster, cheaper and more accessible communications technologies, virtual teams are springing up everywhere — and this workplace trend is increasing.

What works well with conventional teams also works well with virtual or "geographically dispersed" teams: Having a clear purpose and goals, shared roles, open and clear communication, effective decision making, balanced participation, valued diversity, constructively managed conflict, a cooperative climate, etc.

For a virtual team to be successful, each team member must recognize and accommodate the inherent differences when they no longer work face to face. They must pay particular attention to:

Purpose. Virtual teams often operate with a lack of routine policies and procedures. The interactions can be brief and sporadic. Spend some time up front defining and agreeing to the team's mission, vision and goals. This allows team members to get focused quickly, to work with the same purpose and, when lost or distracted, to get back on track.

Prior to each virtual meeting, have an agenda with decision points carefully identified. Do the bulk of the work outside the meeting structure and come prepared to talk about updates or problems.

Communications. We are all familiar with conventional team sessions such as face-to-face meetings, workshops, seminars, presentations and briefings and enabling technology such as photocopiers, fax machines, telephones, voice-mail and e-mail distribution lists. Virtual teams cannot take their communications for granted. They should discuss and agree on the method and frequency of communication.

Virtual teams effectively interact with each other using a variety of methods: audio conference calls, videoconferences, online conversations, interactive digital meetings and conferences, intranets, and the Internet. The cost of using "high tech" communications media is falling dramatically. What you once thought wasn't possible or affordable may now be an option, so check it out!

Miscommunication. Accept the inevitability of a communication misfire, especially if the team does not know each other well. Conflict can escalate as remote team members read between the lines. On the other hand, some teams report *less* conflict due to the equalizing influence of technology. In cyberspace, all ideas are heard.

People. The good news is that virtual team members can come from anywhere — so you can have the right people on the team. Everyone should be an expert in something needed to accomplish the work. They should be well versed in team skills, self-motivated and highly independent. The result is that you have a professional team representing a wide diversity of knowledge and skills.

Most virtual teams need some face-to-face time together to function effectively, especially at the beginning to agree on purpose and communication methods as well as to understand and appreciate each other. Be flexible and open to new ideas and methods, learning what works best. Come together again at critical milestones to realign the work and celebrate small successes. You'll find that your team will become more virtual over time.

Chapter Seven

Houston, We Have A Problem...

Even though you have set your team up for success by planning and preparing for a great team session, problems are inevitable. It's like death and taxes. You can count on them!

So approach problems as an opportunity for the *team* to learn and grow. Even though it appears one person is causing all the trouble, it's the *team's* responsibility to turn the "problem" behavior around. When the team resolves the issue, they emerge with a better understanding of how to work together better as a team.

This chapter will focus on dealing with typical problem situations.

Every problem is an opportunity...

Manage the Inevitable Conflicts

Most people dislike conflict. Rather than express disagreement, they will avoid the issue or withdraw from the conversation. On the other hand, some thrive on conflict and the thrill of victory, bullying their issue until they "win."

Conflict is a normal part of your team's development, creativity and productivity. Managed effectively, conflict enables the team to communicate its differences, seek common goals and build a collaborative consensus or "win/win." Managed ineffectively, conflict can lead to frustration, stonewalling, and a breakdown in your team's work.

When your team members have different ideas or interests, take the time to manage the conflict constructively:

Just Listen. Let the conflicted parties talk completely and without interruption. Actively listen to what they have to say. Try to understand why they are so intent on getting their way. Mentally separate the specific facts and issues from their position.

Reassure. Check your understanding of their perspective. Do not imply either of your perspectives is right or wrong. Let them know they have a right to feel the way they do. Validate their feelings but don't mirror their emotions! Stay neutral. Don't let their anger or excitement affect your voice, tone, body language or words. (A word to the wise: If after lots of listening and reassuring, they still haven't calmed down, suggest that you take a break and return at a specific time to continue the discussion.) Emotions just add fuel to the fire.

Build Trust. Agree on what the conflict is. Let them know you would like to see the conflict resolved and that you are willing to work toward a mutually beneficial solution. It is absolutely critical that you are honest and you believe the conflict can be resolved. Be truthful and don't manipulate the situation for your own benefit. Avoid using the words, "Yes, but." Use "I agree and."

Look for the Win/Win. As you work through major issues of the conflict, take the time to summarize both or all sides. Then summarize where you agree and disagree. Continue to listen and empathize, focusing on solving the conflict. By moving past the positions and identifying the underlying issues, agree on a mutually acceptable solution to resolve the conflict. Make suggestions for moving forward and agree on what each of you will do next. Take time to plan positive, practical and concrete steps you both can take. Be sure to write these down so all can remember what was promised.

End with the Future. Summarize your understanding and let them know what you will do, what you expect them to do, and by when. Close with a check-in to make sure they are "okay" and the conflict has been resolved or plan the next time you will get together.

Most disagreements can be settled in a single session and have no need to progress further. In this way, you can increase the quality of the team's work and decisions by looking for solutions that meet everyone's objectives.

Common Disruptive Behaviors

Each individual comes to the team with an agenda. When each person's agenda coincides with the team's agenda, no problem! However, when one person's agenda is out of whack with the team's, you now have a "hidden agenda" or a "disruptive" team member.

While easy to ignore in the beginning, these behaviors continue to build, creating resentment within the team. At the beginning of each team meeting, prevent disruptions by agreeing on team ground rules. Make sure team members share the responsibility for reinforcing the ground rules.

When disruptive behaviors keep the team from moving forward, remind the team of the ground rules. If the behavior persists, privately give constructive feedback to focus their behaviors in more appropriate ways.

For the most part, people don't want to disrupt the team's progress. When a disruptive behavior occurs, ask questions directed toward the behavior and not the person. Clarifying the cause of the behavior contributes to effective communications and will enable everyone to identify, relate to and understand whatever it takes to keep the team functioning effectively.

Here are some common disruptive roles and behaviors:

"The Attacker" deflates the spirits of other team members by criticizing them. Establish a ground rule to attack issues and not the person. Ask the attacker to summarize both sides of the issue. Intervene if he attacks and remind him of the ground rule.

"The Clown" ridicules others, making jokes at the expense of others. A little humor can be a great asset to

the team, but the clown goes overboard. Redirect the clown's attention with serious questions. If the behavior persists, appeal to the comedian to balance the team's work and have a good time as well.

"The Cynic" opposes the team and disagrees beyond reason. Ask her to share the "whys" of her perspective. Use light-hearted humor to point out the negativity. Challenge the team to find ways around the problem.

"The Dominator" monopolizes airtime. Establish a ground rule to balance participation such as "all participate...no one dominates." Avoid eye contact to discourage the dominator from continuing the monologue.

"The Interrupter" constantly interrupts the speaker or starts side conversations with other team members. Establish ground rules such as "no side conversations" or "one person speaks at a time." Stand your ground when they interrupt; hold your hand up and say, "I'd like to continue..."

"The Loner" withdraws by being aloof, silent or indifferent. Ask open-ended questions to invite their participation. Draw them into the discussion by going around the room asking for input. Ask each team member to write his or her ideas down on paper first. Get the loner involved by asking them to post charts on the wall, keep time, hand out materials, etc.

"The Movie Star" craves attention. The star boasts and tells others about their accomplishments. To minimize distractions, be attentive before and after the team meetings and during breaks. During the meeting, give the movie star something to keep her occupied, such as recording the discussion.

"**The Prisoner**" is forced to be on the team. Turn the prisoner's resentment to a beneficial "reality check" for the team. Link his work to business results and performance. Over time, the prisoner will realize the benefits to being part of the team.

"**The Last Word**" has to have the last word on a topic. Give everyone two poker chips and call them "last word chips." Anyone on the team can use one of the chips when they want the last word. No new chips are distributed until everyone has had a turn at having the last word.

The Chronic Latecomer

A common team problem is getting people to meetings on time. Meetings start late, people straggle in, and they are distracted with other activities.

Try these techniques to tackle this pesky problem:

Start on Time. If the meeting was supposed to start at 8 a.m., start at 8 a.m. regardless. No matter who is missing. Even the big banana. If you don't, you simply reinforce tardiness.

Be Odd. Schedule your session to start at an odd time e.g. 8:07 am. People will be more likely to remember an odd time and make an effort to be there.

Be Convenient. Schedule your session at a convenient time and place for the majority of the team members.

Be Comfortable. An attractive meeting room with comfortable chairs is much more enticing than a cinder block cell (oops, I meant conference room).

Have Food. People like to go places where there is free food. Even having cold sodas on hand can boost attendance!

Close the Door when the meeting begins. If they know they can't "slip in" late, they might just arrive on time!

Schedule Priorities First. Schedule the important agenda items for the beginning of the meeting. Better yet, schedule the important items of interest to the chronic latecomer first — so it's in the latecomer's self-interest to be on time.

Pressure 'Em. Ask the team for help in dealing with the chronic latecomers. Peer pressure works wonders.

Shame Them. Publish the names of absentees and latecomers in the team minutes.

Describe Consequences. If you are the latecomer's supervisor, describe the consequences of the tardiness. If not, then go get "horsepower" to encourage them to be on time.

Levels of Intervention

Highest   Mediate
Discuss Online
Discuss Off-Line with "Horsepower"
Discuss Off-Line

Process Check
Feedback to the Team
Park It
Remind
Limit Air-Time
Make a Suggestion
Redirect

Combine Eye Contact and Movement
Movement
Lowest   Eye Contact

Gracefully Handle Disruptive Team Members

For the most part, people who are being disruptive don't realize the impact they are having on the team; they are just being themselves. The key to handling these situations is to intervene gracefully while maintaining the self-esteem of the disrupter.

When intervening, you want to use the lowest, most non-threatening level possible. Start with:

Make Eye Contact with the disrupter. If that doesn't work, escalate to the next level.

Move. Make some kind of movement toward the disrupter. If sitting, lean forward. If standing, step toward the person.

Combine the Two. Use eye contact and movement at the same time, usually with a small touch of the dramatic.

Redirect. Turn the disrupter's comments into a constructive contribution to the team's discussion. Suggest a new viewpoint or angle on the situation.

Make a Suggestion. Ask a leading question to invite the group to proceed in a more constructive direction.

Limit Air Time. Direct the discussion away from the disrupter by asking questions or brainstorming around the table.

Remind the team of the ground rules and/or the agenda established at the beginning of the meeting.

Park It. If the team can proceed without resolving the issue, "park it" by agreeing to come back to it later. Often times, the issue becomes irrelevant as the meeting progresses.

FeedBack. Using the rules of feedback, give the team some specific, behavioral observations — without judgment.

Process Check. Ask the team to step back from the discussion, and talk about the process. Then ask a question that focuses on the process, not the content of the discussion, e.g. "What might be in the way of the team coming to agreement?"

If the behavior continues, you may choose to escalate your intervention to an even higher level:

Off-Line. At the next break, talk to the disrupter one-on-one. Describe the disruptive behavior and the impact on the team. Reach agreement on how to move forward.

Off-Line with Horsepower. If time permits, ask the team leader or team sponsor to talk to the disrupter one-on-one.

Online. In front of the team, discreetly point out the behavior, and ask for cooperation.

Mediate. In situations involving conflict, ask for the entire team's help in resolving the problem. Go through a formal process to define the problem and brainstorm possible solutions for a win/win. Avoid further disruptions by confirming agreement on how to move forward.

Keep in mind that you aren't alone. There are probably others on your team who will appreciate — and even assist — your attempts to handle the problem. Call on these people as allies to move the meeting forward.

Finally, when a serious disruption occurs, be patient and remain calm — no matter how emotional you feel about the problem or the disrupter. Don't add fuel to the fire and let the problem pass by. You will be in a better position to deal with the problem later, when all parties are cool, clear and level-headed!

Intervene Off-Line

Occasionally, one particular team member is keeping the team from making progress. You have tried to gracefully intervene, using escalating levels of interventions. But the disrupter still doesn't get it. This one person is the source of the team's inability to proceed.

You *must* talk with this person about his or her performance. However, team leaders and team members will avoid confronting the issue or the person and will attempt all kinds of ways to deal with the problem indirectly. Unfortunately, none of these approaches work well.

To successfully resolve the situation:

Be Direct and to the point. If you have a problem, say so directly to the person, using the rules of feedback.

Be Specific about what the problem is. State the facts as you see it.

Stay Cool. Be positive in your tone and non-verbals. Angry, accusatory behavior will make the other person defensive and compelled to justify their actions.

Be Silent. Ask, "What happened?" in an open, non-accusatory tone of voice. Give the other person a chance to respond. Listen and do not interrupt. Ask questions to clarify what the other person said.

You have now brought the problem to the surface. Continue to Build Trust, Look for the Win/Win and End with the Future as described in *Manage the Inevitable Conflicts* on pages 156-7.

Intervene Off-Line with Horsepower

You have tried to resolve the issue on-on-one; however, the disruptive member is not cooperating. If time permits, call on the "horsepower" — those folks "up the food chain" that can influence the disrupter's behavior. The team champion, team member supervisors or a highly respected authority may just be able to provide the insight the disrupter needs to become productive.

As you appeal to these key influential people to intervene on behalf of the team:

Be Very Specific. Tell the influencers what has happened and what you need for them to do. For example: "For the last four meetings, John has arrived fifteen minutes late to the meeting and has not completed his tasks assigned. This is keeping the team from achieving our goal on time. Could you please speak with him and let him know just how important his contribution is? We really need him to be on time and to come prepared."

Keep It Simple. Don't overwhelm them with details, just limit your discussion to the facts. Otherwise, your "horsepower" may get sucked into the melodrama, trying to guess what really happened.

Get Commitment. Ask for their help and support in correcting this disruptive behavior as soon as possible.

End on a Positive Note. Reaffirm the strengths the member brings to the team and how you want to see the issue resolved.

Mediate Conflict

You have done your best. The conflict has now escalated to the point where the team is generating "heat" about the issue. A conflict between two or more separate parties is best resolved through a negotiation or "mediation" process. To resolve the disagreement:

Halt the Process. Stop the conversation. Provide feedback to both parties that the issue has gotten out of hand. Involve the entire team to discover a win-win resolution of the issue. Suggest a mediation process to move forward.

Agree to Proceed. Once the team has committed to finding a solution, give a brief overview of the mediation process and suggest a few ground rules:

- ❏ Be a good listener. Listen as an ally, not an adversary.

- ❏ One person speaks at a time.

- ❏ Let's generate "light" around this issue, rather than "heat."

- ❏ Be open to another point of view.

What Is the Problem? Ask each person (or divide into sub-teams) to describe the problem from each point of view. Ask: What does "A" want or need? What does "B" want or need? Each party is questioned while the other listens, asking questions only for clarification.

Is There a Problem? After the questioning, the parties verify there is, indeed, a problem. The team just might be in "violent agreement" over the same issue! If not, agree on a mutual definition and understanding of the problem.

Areas of Agreement. Brainstorm the things the two (or more) positions have in common.

Areas of Disagreement. Brainstorm the disagreements between the two positions. You may discover the disagreements are trivial and the team can move forward easily.

Look for the Win/Win. Have each party (or sub-team) brainstorm solutions that could satisfy both parties. Look for agreement or close agreement in their solutions. Clarify, combine and synergize to build a consensus — a decision that everyone can live with and support.

End with the Future. Summarize the team's understanding of the agreed upon solution. Agree on next steps to move forward.

Balance Participation

In today's meaner, leaner and more sophisticated workplace, employees want and expect to be able to contribute to the job, not just "check their brains at the door."

For whatever reason, perhaps your team just isn't participating. It might be because it has always been that way, team members don't know any different, they have tried to participate and were unsuccessful, or they simply choose not to. Keep in mind that whatever happened in the past is history.

Be Frank. Start your next meeting with a frank conversation about how you feel about their participation. Give them specific observations about their participation at your staff meetings. While you do this, don't criticize, question or make them feel bad about their behavior.

Seek First to Understand. Ask some open-ended questions to understand where they are coming from. For example: "What do you think about what I am saying?" Listen to what they have to say — you might be surprised at what you hear.

Discuss Possible Strategies. Discuss the following strategies for increasing their participation:

- ❑ Volunteer ideas, suggestions and information willingly and without finality.

- ❑ Use a round-robin technique to gain input from all participants.

- ❑ Encourage input from quieter team members. Make eye contact and ask if anyone else has a comment or question.

- ❑ Ask for and listen to all points of view.

- ❏ Listen to one another without interrupting or completing others' sentences.

- ❏ Make positive remarks about other team members and their contributions.

- ❏ Refer to team members by name.

- ❏ Break the team into smaller groups and then have the groups report to the larger team.

- ❏ Encourage and reinforce new and creative ideas.

- ❏ Do not tolerate side-tracking, hidden agendas or domination.

- ❏ Summarize your understanding of what others have said.

Agree on New Ground Rules. As a team, identify the top three strategies to increase your team's participation. Add these three strategies to your team ground rules. Reassure them that you want to emphasize these three strategies, and then encourage the behavior.

For the Team Leader: After you have discussed these strategies, let team members know that it is not just your responsibility as "boss" to do all these things...but that it is every team member's responsibility. As the leader, make the extra effort to "do" the three strategies. Your employees will be looking to you as a role model, and to see if you really want their participation.

Keep in mind however, that talking is not necessarily a measure of participation. We all know people who talk a lot and say nothing. Look for opportunities to create the environment where each individual contributes when appropriate.

Follow the Leader

I have a baseball cap with the words "Obey Me" written across the top. It's part of a team activity in which the participants may choose to follow the instructions on various hats placed on team member's heads.

Invariably, everyone follows the leader with the "Obey Me" hat — whether the "leader" wants them to or not.

This tendency to defer to the leader weakens the team's work. The team is missing out on worthwhile contributions. Decisions are essentially "done deals." No one feels particularly satisfied with the end result. Try these techniques to overcome the "obey me" syndrome:

Go Around. When asking for input, go around the table and make sure everyone's opinions are heard.

Write It Down. Some people like to think about the topic before they answer, so let them write their thoughts on a piece of paper and then share them.

Comment Anonymously. Ask the team to write their thoughts on stickie notes — one idea per stickie. Then have the team members randomly post the notes on a flipchart. Stand back and see what ideas emerge.

Write It Up. As each team member offers an opinion, record what they say on a flipchart for all to see. Make sure you use their words, rather than project your interpretation.

Go Last. Offer your opinion after everyone else has had the opportunity to speak. Integrate your comments with others.

Go First. Before the discussion begins, let people know you want frank discussion. Make it OK for the team to challenge your assumptions and point of view.

Aim for Unanimity. If you want to avoid the "dashboard dog effect" — heads bobbing up and down in apparent agreement with you — strive for unanimity where everyone must agree on the result. Don't settle for compromises or half-hearted agreements.

Leave. If you think your presence is keeping the team from speaking up, leave the room and give the team the freedom to discuss the issues.

The Problem Is Bigger Than All of Us

Sometimes you just don't know what is going on with the team. It's not just one person. It's more than just a few people. Everybody feels a certain way and you just can't pinpoint what the problem is.

The best way to deal with team problems, particularly those which are "unspoken," is to create a safe space to talk about them. The group may show some "symptoms" of team trouble:

Confusion. If the team appears confused as to what they are supposed to be doing, chances are it lacks "vision," a clear understanding of the goal or end state. Clarify the goal until everyone can visualize the mission accomplished.

Lack of Integrity. If the team is saying one thing and yet doing another, or the behavior borders on the unacceptable, chances are they have a misalignment of team values. Have a brutally frank discussion on what is acceptable and unacceptable behavior. Make the team's values explicitly known to each team member. Agree on how the behaviors will be enforced. What will happen if someone breaks a team ground rule? Agree to hold each other accountable and not look the other way.

Diffusion. If each team member appears to be doing "their own thing," chances are the team strategy is not in place. Decide how the team is going to accomplish the task, who is going to do what, and by when.

Frustration. If the team appears frustrated, chances are the team lacks the resources to do the job properly. Either get the resources or modify the job expectations with the limited resources you have.

Fatigue. If the team appears to be tired and it is hard to get them moving, excited and alive, chances are you have a problem with motivation or capability. Probe deeper to find the cause of the problem. It may be a training, skills or knowledge issue or a lack of interest.

Doubt. Finally, if the team doubts that their work will make a difference, chances are they need feedback from management on how their work contributes to the organization's overall success.

Symptom	You're Missing
Confusion	Vision
Lack of Integrity	Values
Diffusion	Strategy
Frustration	Resources
Fatigue	Capability or Motivation
Doubt	Feedback

Some Teams Just Don't Want To Die

At one time, it may have been a high performing team — doing great work with great people. But now...it's different...it's not the same...it's not as fun as it once was. It's a real challenge for teams to know when they should simply say "goodbye."

Look for these signs that your team's work is done:

You're Done. Your team has accomplished the mission. Hooray! Congratulate yourselves on a job well done. Make sure there are sufficient structures in place to ensure the issue won't come up again. Watch out for the team that goes "searching" for a new mission — just to keep the team together.

No Customer. Take a look at what your team has been chartered to do. Who is the customer and/or end user of that final product? Sometimes the customer isn't there, doesn't care, wasn't ever there and won't ever be there. If you don't have a customer for your team product, no one is going to "buy" it and your team doesn't need to exist.

Below Critical Mass. How many people were on the team when it was chartered? Now how many are on board? Sure, team members come and go, but watch out when critical expertise is not replaced. There is such a thing as "critical mass" which varies from team to team — the minimum needed to get the job done. When the team is at or below critical mass and cannot perform its functions any longer, it's time for the team to stop the lunacy. Get more help or disband the team.

Just Can't Do It. I realize everyone is operating on a shoestring and you can't always get what you want. But your team should be able to get what it needs. If your team literally cannot do its job without a specific resource (be creative — how did they do it ten, twenty or thirty years ago?), then go get it. Like a dog, rabidly pursue it. If still you can't get it, stop beating each other up and call it a day.

Floating in Space. Every team should have someone in management who is championing their efforts. The champion removes barriers to team success and provide resources as needed. In the event the team loses its champion (e.g. job transfer, other priorities, or death), the team needs to find a new champion to link the team's efforts to business strategy. Otherwise, the lifeline has been cut and the team is just floating out in space.

Enough Already. The team has been in existence forever. The same people have been on the team. They have been working on the same project. They are tired, burned out, and need to move on. There seems to be no end in sight. Like a fatally wounded animal, just put it out of its misery.

In many cases, the team wants so desperately to stay together, it ignores these signs. It takes on a life of its own finding busy work and not really accomplishing meaningful results.

The first step is to recognize the signs and then have a discussion with the team. Often times, it's simply a matter of regrouping your energies and accessing the right people or resources. Maybe it is time for the team to move on. Listen to people as they share their opinions and feelings. Recognize that there will be a wide range of emotions: glad, sad, worried, excited. Reach agreement on the future of the team and ensure closure for the teams' results and relationships.

Chapter Eight

Special Teams

Every team is special based on the very nature of the charter, the diverse strategies to achieve the goal and the unique contributions of each team member.

This chapter focuses on the unique characteristics and challenges of some common types of teams:

- ❑ Cross-functional teams
- ❑ Generational teams
- ❑ Implementation teams
- ❑ Multi-national teams
- ❑ Process improvement teams
- ❑ Project teams
- ❑ Self-directed teams
- ❑ Staff meetings
- ❑ Strategic planning teams
- ❑ Volunteer board teams

Cross-Functional Teams

Cross-functional teams are typically formed to accomplish organizational or division-wide goals. By their very nature, they call from different specialties, disciplines, departments or "functions" within the organization.

As you charter cross-functional teams, consider:

Cost to Benefit. Will this team actually provide greater benefit than the costs involved? Factor in the salaries, benefits, lost time, materials required, etc.

Membership. Having the right people on the team is absolutely imperative to its success. I believe this is the number one cause of failure.

Representation. Keep in mind that team members are selected for their expertise, their ability to work with others and their ability to represent their fellow workers. Make sure you provide an "accordion process" for each team member to solicit ideas and feedback as the team makes progress.

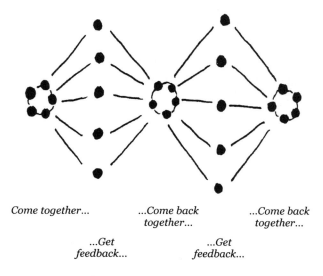

Come together...   ...Come back   ...Come back
                          together...   together...

        ...Get   ...Get
     feedback...   feedback...

Time Requirements. Will the team be expected to work full-time or part-time? How many hours will be expected to be devoted to the team? Will overtime be available and under what specific conditions?

Work Load. What happens to the work the team members were doing that will no longer get done as a result of this project? Are team members expected to adjust their priorities, or will they be expected to accomplish the same amount of work *plus* the teamwork, regardless? If relieved of all their current duties and assigned to the team full-time, what will happen to them upon successful completion of the project? (Hopefully, they will be rewarded with a "good" job and reinserted where they can continue to spread the team philosophy...).

Supervisory Relationships. Team members will be doing work outside of their normal workplace. How will the team members keep their supervisors and fellow workers informed? How will their efforts be incorporated into their performance reviews?

Champion. Every cross-functional team needs a champion or sponsor, someone who can remove roadblocks and provide encouragement to ensure team success (see chapter three).

An consider everything we have talked about in this book including chartering for success, planning for each team session, and improving the process each time the team meets!

Generational Teams

Often characterized as being lazy, arrogant, unreliable, and cynical, Generation X is considered to be anything BUT team-oriented. Or so thought Hank Karp and Danilo Sirias, professors in the Department of Management and Marketing at Christopher Newport University. They conducted a pilot study of 398 people from six organizations across the country and concluded that Generation X is significantly *more* team-oriented than the Baby Boomers!

How could this be? How can Xers, who are known to be extremely independent and prefer to work on a task alone, value teamwork? Karp and Sirias suggest that Xer's are looking for "valuable teams which support the individual" rather than the Boomer's mantra that "the team is an entity greater than the sum of its parts." Rather than being a "melting pot," teams of the future will look more like a "salad bowl," where each individual makes the best contribution to the team effort.

As a result, teamwork is evolving to a higher and more challenging standard. For an Xer, a high performing team is composed of strong, diverse individuals, focused on delivering results, who create flexible linkages to work as an entire team, in isolation or in different configurations depending on the task. They are looking for authentic team synergy rather than conformance to group norms.

The good news is Boomers and Xers actually have a common approach to teamwork. However, as more Xers enter the workplace, Boomers will have to learn how to value individual diversity, manage conflict, motivate individuals and delegate tasks much more effectively. Karp and Sirias recommend the following strategies as you bring Generation Xers onto your team:

Identify Strengths and Interests of team members before integrating them into an effective and cohesive work unit.

Encourage Individual Identity. Today's teams tend to focus on the group identity as the primary means of identifying the individual members. Make a greater effort to recognize individual strengths, contributions and achievements.

Integrate Perspectives. Boomers see their primary individual role as supporting the team while the Xers see the team's primary function as supporting individual efforts and relationships. Both perspectives must be discussed as the team moves forward.

Coach and Provide Personal Support with individual members. Karp and Sirias theorize the majority of Xers had two parents working during their formative years. To make up for this lack of attention, Xers have a need for closer personalized contact with those above them.

Focus on Results. Xers, as a group, appear to be much more pragmatic. They will forge linkages to work on task subsections individually and then bring the results to the team. Team issues will be dealt with more easily when cast within the context of achieving team objectives.

Motivate with the Work. Xers are not going to be motivated by appeals to the greater good, loyalty to the organization, or allusions to the "Big Picture." Motivation comes from within and has to do with the intrinsic nature of the team's work.

Reward Team *and* Individual Contribution. The current practice is to reward the team as a whole, rather than single out any one individual on the team. However, Xers are much more tuned in to "what's in it for me" (WIIFM). Test out different ways to reward individual contributions to the team.

Implementation Teams

Implementation teams are chartered to implement a specific plan of action. Typically a cross-functional team, the team has been brought together to carry out someone else's decision.

As you charter an implementation team to carry out your plan:

Tell 'Em Everything. Let the team know why, what, who, where, how and by when. They were not part of the decision-making process, so they have no ownership nor buy-in to the decision. By telling them everything you know, and allowing for a healthy question and answer period, you will foster a greater sense of commitment and interest.

Paint the Picture. Describe the end state, the project accomplished, success achieved so there is no doubt what the goal is.

Tap Into their WIIFM (What's In It For Me). Your success is highly dependent on how motivated and committed the team is to achieving results. Make a great case for why they should make this team successful. Then ask: What's in it for each team member. You might be surprised at their answers! (Hint: it's not just about money...)

Measure Progress. Create a visual display to track team progress. Don't forget to keep it up to date and refer to it often. This stimulates progress and allows the team to know that there is light at the end of the tunnel.

Be Flexible. No plan ever runs smoothly. So roll with the punches, accept a few steps backward and leaps forward, as long as the team is making progress toward implementation.

Be Demanding. Set high expectations. Communicate your expectations frequently and regularly. Don't waiver from the goal. But also balance your demands with the reality that the goals were set high in the first place.

It's an interesting team dynamic: Teams strive to reach a goal but rarely do they surpass it. For example, if you charter a team to reduce cycle time by 30 percent, the team will be delighted with anything around the 30-ish ballpark (20-29 percent). They'll be ecstatic with anything *over* 30.

But if you really need a 30 percent reduction, aim for 40 percent.

Multi-National Teams

Teams with members from several nations have a unique way of communicating, building consensus and taking action. If you're sponsoring a multinational team, there are several measures you can take to ensure teamwork:

Do Your Research. Know who will be participating and what they will expect. If possible, ask for their opinions from the beginning. Know their names and proper titles.

Provide "Read-Ahead" Packages. These will include detailed information about the agenda and the team's goals. Many are not accustomed to the direct "American-style" meeting, so make sure you clue them in on the process the team will use.

Be Balanced. Have different nationalities co-lead the team to ensure equal representation. Handouts should be multi-lingual. Explain what the team's products will be — recommendation, project plan, etc. Use a storyboard to reinforce where the team is and where it needs to go.

Define Key Words. Pay particular attention to phrases that may not translate well. For example, "one conversation at a time" may mean to some members "don't talk to more than one person at a time." Clarify the language if the team members seem confused or do something unexpected. Use simple diagrams as much as possible.

Be Culturally Sensitive. Every person on the team brings his or her own set of assumptions, values and beliefs. What works well in one country may not work well in another. For example, the French like to take long lunches whereas Americans are used to working lunches. Americans openly question everything, whereas Japanese will question in private.

Learn About Their Cultures. Because a multi-national team has many dimensions to consider, learn about the members' cultures before you jump to conclusions. Take the time to learn a few words in their language, some customs, the country's geography, and even a typical meal.

Schedule Free Time. Plan some sightseeing or a trip to an ethnic restaurant to help the team bond. A series of low-key activities often is more useful for getting the group to coalesce than one "grand slam." Be sensitive to cultural norms regarding diet or inclusion of spouses and children.

Don't Assume...

Don't assume that people have the same views about 'teamwork.' Early on in the team's formation, discuss the key elements to building an extraordinary team. Explore:

❑ What do you mean by the word "team?"

❑ How do you expect this team to function?

❑ What should be our ground rules for team effectiveness?

Process Improvement Teams

Want to improve a process within your organization? Gather all the people who touch the process — those who are involved in the activities within the process boundaries (the start and end points). Make sure you have a representative of each step in the process on the team.

Agree on the Process Improvement Goal. To reduce cycle time, reduce waste, reduce costs, increase customer satisfaction. If this is your first improvement effort, start with a small, worthwhile project. Agree on how you are going to improve the process, and how long the process should take. If you need management support, resources or training, ask for them.

Flowchart the Current Process by brainstorming all the steps to the process. The best way to do this is to write each step on a separate stickie note and then arrange the steps in chronological order. Some teams literally walk the product through the process, simultaneously documenting the process flow and cycle time. Make sure the team documents how the process actually occurs — not how it should be!

Identify the Waste. From this common understanding of the work process, identify the redundancies, duplication of effort, non-value added work or loopbacks. Most of the waste in a process occurs in the hand-offs between steps, often called "the white space."

Simplify the Process by fixing the obvious problems, or "low hanging fruit." A team typically improves a process by up to 50 percent just by flowcharting and simplifying the process! Don't forget to communicate and implement these simple changes to all affected.

Want to improve the process even more? For many problems, the Pareto Principle applies: 80 percent of the trouble comes from 20 percent of the problems. Find out what causes the problem, and you've solved the majority of your problems!

Identify Possible Root Causes. Ask why the problem occurs. Keep asking why until you discover a common pattern, theme or trend. Most root causes can be categorized into five areas: machinery, manpower, materials, methods or environment.

Rather than relying on your team's gut instinct, validate the most probable root cause (or causes) with data. If you don't have the data on hand, then organize how to collect the data with checklists, checksheets, surveys, trend charts or other data collection methods. Collect the information and then analyze it for root causes using Pareto charts, trend charts, and other analytical tools.

Brainstorm Possible Solutions to the root cause. Be creative and innovative! Agree on a solution (or solutions) that will dramatically improve your process.

Develop and Implement a Plan to test the changes. Check to see if you achieved the team's improvement goal. If not, then redesign improvements to the process.

If your team reaches its goal, standardize the new process and celebrate the team's success! Provide an opportunity to share what went well and what they might do differently. In this way, the team can improve its own improvement process!

Process Improvement Versus Re-engineering

Many organizations banter about the terms "process improvement" and "re-engineering" loosely, without really understanding their meaning.

Many of these "programs" are based on management philosophies centered on systems thinking and the impact on the quality of the product or service. While many of these concepts have been around for some time, Dr. W. Edwards Deming, Dr. Joseph Juran and Philip Crosby popularized "TQM" or Total Quality Management in the 1980s.

In a nutshell, TQM is a way of running an organization that focuses its efforts in a systematic, disciplined fashion on improving continuously the quality of everything it does. By learning how to monitor, control, and constantly improve their systems, organizations are better able to provide customers with what they want, when and how they want it. TQM is not a "program," but an overall systematic way of managing.

The confusion comes in when companies decide *how* they are going to achieve ever-increasing levels of quality, gain a competitive edge and be profitable.

Problem Solving Teams take a problem and fix it.

Process Improvement Teams make small, incremental improvements to a process by streamlining, reducing waste, eliminating duplication and preventing problems from happening in the first place. All of which, if done properly, can yield significant results.

But if the system is broken, process improvement won't yield large breakthrough results. Michael Hammer popularized *re-engineering* which uses technology as an enabler to create new processes and systems, based on customer requirements.

The critical difference with re-engineering and *renovating* a process is that re-engineering starts with the customer requirements, and the team then re-engineers (or reinvents, creates, or innovates) a brand new process or system, using information technology. Renovating a process involves major improvements to a process, while maintaining the basic infrastructure of the system.

The genesis of these strategies is in TQM, and depending on what your organization is dealing with, it may opt for a problem-solving, process improvement, renovation or re-engineering strategy. Some take a slightly different path with an intense *focus on the customer* where substantial customer information drives the appropriate management strategy.

A critical difference among the strategies is the time it takes to provide a payback, and the amount of "risk" involved:

Problem Solving paybacks are almost immediate and the risk is small.

Process Improvement paybacks are fast and the risk is small to moderate.

Renovation paybacks are slow and the risk is moderate.

Re-engineering paybacks are either almost immediate or highly delayed, and the risk is high.

It could be that your company has several of these strategies running at the same time. Be involved in how the business leadership integrates the team approach depending on the situation they face. The challenge is to retain focus, commitment, and the courage to see the strategy achieved.

Project Teams

Project teams are typically commissioned to implement a specific project or plan. To set your project team up for success, follow these steps to success:

Craft A Solid Charter. Regardless of whether you have a large or small project, make sure your team has a solid charter from management. This one-page charter typically describes the problem or opportunity the project is to address, the project goal or final deliverable, project objectives or major pieces of work to be done, the criteria for success and a list of any assumptions, risks or obstacles expected.

Make sure you have the right people and expertise on your team — these are the folks who will be responsible for implementing the plan. Try to limit the core group to fewer than twelve; you can invite others to participate on an "as needed" basis. Review the charter and ensure understanding and agreement before you move forward.

Construct a Work Breakdown Structure (WBS). List all the activities needed to be done in order to achieve the project goal. Decide what level of detail your team expects or is necessary to manage the project. The level of detail increases as the project becomes more complex, especially with respect to time and resources required.

Build a "Level One" WBS. Identify the major activities or "chunks" of work that need to be accomplished. For most projects, list no more than ten major activities. Then brainstorm all the tasks that need to be done and place them under the appropriate major activity. Next, sequence the tasks for each major activity and add any items or details that might be missing.

Estimate the Time to complete each task and the resources required (people, facilities, equipment, material, money).

Hint: If the project is complex, develop "work packages," discrete tasks accomplished by a specific trade group or element, typically no more than 80 hours each.

Put each work package or level one task with a time estimate on a stickie note. Ask: "What tasks can be done today?" These tasks have no predecessors. Then ask: "What items have to start when the previous items finish?" Move the stickies next to each other on a horizontal timeline. Draw a connecting line *in pencil*. It will change! Note the relationships with a "node" or dot at connection points and arrows to show direction.

Look at the Big Picture. Can you achieve the goal within the appropriate amount of time and resource constraints? For most teams, the initial answer is "No!" Take a closer look at the project, analyzing what is critical to accomplishing the goal as well as resources required. Can you meet the project on time and within budget? If not, strategize on how to compress the critical timeline, use resources better, define what is critical versus "nice to have" and insert lead and lag times between related tasks.

At this point in the process, teamwork is vital. Listen closely to the issues and look for small agreements on how the work should be done. Continue to analyze the plan until you can meet the project goal or make the goal more realistic!

Remember: A plan is only as good as the effort expended. The ultimate goal is not to produce a glossy, professionally printed plan. The value is that the team has gone through the process of understanding what needs to be done, by whom, and by when — so that the team can achieve the project goal.

Self-Directed Teams

A self-directed or self-managed work team is a small group of five to fifteen people who share responsibility for a particular task. Self-directed teams (SDTs) are responsible and accountable to the business leadership for certain standards of performance. Within well-defined boundaries, they have the authority to plan, implement, monitor and control their processes. They often set their own standards for quality and productivity. They have direct, immediate access to whatever information, resources and training they need to accomplish their objectives.

What makes self-directed teams different from other teams is the level of responsibility and authority that members have for tasks which are typically performed by a supervisor or manager. They work with a minimum of direct supervision, and the leadership role is shared within the team. Each person has an equal voice and opportunity to participate, contribute and decide the team's work. Members of SDTs typically handle job assignments, plan and schedule work, make production-related decisions, and take action on problems.

SDTs are different from quality circles, process action teams and cross-functional task groups in that SDTs are formal, permanent organizational structures. They operate with fewer layers of management. Due to the nature of the work, team members learn all the tasks that need to be performed.

Team members are also responsible for handling the people-related issues traditionally performed by management. They:

❑ Track their own attendance and hours.

❑ Schedule vacations, time off, and overtime.

❑ Deal with conflicts and personality clashes within the group.

❑ Identify and address training needs, and in some cases, train each other.

❑ Identify requirements for new members, select individuals, and hire them.

❑ Evaluate the team's abilities to work together.

❑ Conduct individual performance appraisals within the team.

Self-direction is the highest evolution of team work. It requires a gradual shift toward sharing responsibility, decision-making and information. Business leaders must set the boundaries, train their employees, let go of control, delegate responsibility and authority, and reward team performance. They manage through planning the overall strategy, coaching, facilitating, supporting and removing barriers to team success.

It is not a "quick fix" strategy and may take up to ten years (if ever) to develop the capabilities and earn the trust and responsibility within the business to be truly "self-directed."

If your company has already made the decision to move to self-directed teams (SDTs), ask "why?"

Identify the underlying reasons to sustain such a radical shift in the way individuals do work: improve quality, increase customer satisfaction, increase productivity and/or team performance, lower costs, reduce management or create a sense of ownership and commitment.

Clarify the team's ultimate responsibilities and management expectations. Management should have a clear picture of where the organization is going and how SDTs will benefit the existing mission, strategy and culture.

With the target clearly in sight, you can begin to work toward creating high performing SDTs.

Set the Stage. The first stage centers around selection, planning and training. Select work units with a high degree of teamwork as the "lead" teams to make the transition. Team members should have strong decision-making, communication and technical skills and be internally motivated and able to work with others. Each work unit develops its own transition plan based on goals, current state of readiness and training, communications linkages, roles and responsibilities. SDT members should clearly understand what the teams will look like and how the teams will progress.

Redesign the Work. Take a hard look at the work the team has been chartered to do. Look at work flow, job design and layout issues as well as the support systems such as compensation, training, hierarchy and appraisal. Redesign the work so that the team controls the *whole* job, including all the work inputs and outputs.

Assume Responsibilities. Team members take on basic job responsibilities including routine tasks and improvements, safety, maintenance, job scheduling and ongoing training. Teams create their own support structures including team mission, roles, goals and ground rules. Team training is critical as the team assumes more managerial responsibilities and supervisors shift into a more facilitative, coaching role. This stage is typically the rockiest as teams and managers learn how to work with and trust each other.

Take on More. The team has demonstrated success, and management is now able to hand off higher level responsibilities, enabling teams to create new ways to solve problems, improve complex processes and respond to their customers. The team also takes on more internal management functions such as hiring employees, tracking attendance, scheduling work and cross training. In this stage, reality starts to sink in; SDTs are responsible and held accountable for their actions.

Get Over the Hump. Everyone starts to see the positive effects of SDTs and is willing to share success stories and failures (lessons learned) with other departments. The teams start to receive more handoffs with the work becoming seamless from one SDT to another. Managers rediscover their reasons for creating SDTs and start comparing "then" to "now." It's an exciting stage where skeptics are now on board and the work starts humming.

Achieve the Goal. Management finally relinquishes the most complex duties. SDTs are expected to conduct performance reviews, coordinate employee recognition, manage the disciplinary process, develop budgets and determine employee compensation. The challenge here is to keep the SDT momentum and continue the team's growth and development.

Developing SDTs requires a high degree of planning, selecting the right team players, designing the work, training continuously and carefully managing the shift of power and responsibilities from supervisors to team members.

Staff Meetings

Staff meetings are a valuable way to communicate information from management, assign or clarify tasks, assess project progress, share information, prevent or solve problems, make decisions and build the team. However, these routine, predictable meetings can suffer from the same weaknesses of any meeting poor preparation, unclear goals or taskings, no agenda, late starts and finishes, etc. The difference is you see the same problems recur again and again!

The good news is that there are some small changes your team can make which will boost your staff meeting productivity:

Meet Weekly. Limit your meetings to once per week. Use technology (e-mail, voice-mail) if you need to communicate more frequently. If you don't have a full agenda, cancel the meeting and move the agenda items to the following week.

Clarify Your Purpose. Staff meetings can quickly degenerate into problem solving among a few people. Keep your purpose in mind, and if you get off track, schedule another meeting with only the right people (maybe right after the staff meeting) to deal with the new issue.

Prepare an Agenda. Because staff meetings are so predictable, teams tend to use the same informal agenda — but seldom follow it! Prepare an agenda *for each meeting,* with specific topics and corresponding team member responsible for that topic. Anticipate obstacles or areas where you'll need more time.

Keep Time. Start on time, end on time. Set time frames on each segment of your meeting. Use a timekeeper who lets the team know when there are five and two minutes to go. When time is up, either renegotiate the agenda, put the discussion on the next week's agenda or drop it. By all means, if you finish a topic early, move on! Everybody likes to end a meeting earlier than expected.

Balance Participation. Supervisors should limit their "airtime" to 50 percent (or lower). This may require some planning/editing of your briefing material. Recognize that some information has to be formally communicated, but frequently check whether or not the information has been covered adequately somewhere else. Distribute routine information prior to the meeting. Encourage input from all team members. Ensure each team member has a role or responsibility.

Follow Up. At the end of each meeting, close with a brief summary of assignments and due dates. Ensure the taskings and key decisions are recorded and carried through to the next appropriate staff meeting. Review all outstanding items at the next staff meeting.

Strategic Planning Teams

Strategic planning teams agree on the purpose and direction of a division or entire organization. Typically, ten to twelve people are selected for their expertise, position within the organization and their ability to represent their peers and the company as a whole.

The strategic planning team will meet to create the strategic plan in three phases: strategic thinking, strategic analysis and long range planning.

Strategic Thinking. Your team will establish or validate your mission, and create the future vision.

Strategic Analysis. Your team will identify the critical issues facing the division by scanning the internal and external environment and gathering information about those issues.

Long Range Planning. Your team will create breakthrough objectives, long range goals, action plans and measures. The strategic action plans then link into the annual operational plan.

Strategic planning is usually completed within a one- or two-month window. Unless you have been released from your daily duties, expect to feel severe pressures that your "regular work" isn't getting done. Much of your time will be spent in the planning meetings, but even more time will be spent in talking with others in the division, getting their ideas, enrolling them to help you collect information and preparing a quick brief on a critical issue.

Many planning sessions are held off-site. Plan to have dinner with your team because much of the creativity and alternative analyses occur in an unstructured environment — and it enhances teamwork!

A Word of Caution. By the end of the day, you may discover that thinking strategically is more tiring than your day-to-day tactical thinking.

A Critical Element. Your division or organization leadership must be personally involved with the strategic planning process. They should have a full understanding, appreciation and commitment to the process, results and resources involved, on a personal as well as an organizational level.

It sounds like a tremendous amount of work, and it is. But if you contribute 100 percent to the process, looking at the long-range future of your organization, many things become clear about current operations. You develop an appreciation for the long-term benefits and short-term payoffs for each activity, as well as a sense of ownership and pride in the future of your division.

Volunteer Board Teams

Volunteer organizations usually have a plethora of boards, committees, task forces and other types of teams to help achieve the organization's mission.

Many of these team members are busy professionals, inspired by the organization's good work. However, when push comes to shove, higher priorities prevail. So, follow these tips to keep your boards from being "bored:"

State Your Expectations. These volunteers have been invited to sit on the board or committee for a specific reason. Maybe it's because of their position within the community, a talent they have to offer, or their willingness to donate time to a worthwhile cause. Whatever the reason, tell them why they are on the board, and what you expect to do with their wonderful abilities. (P.S. It should be more than just attending a meeting now and again).

Be Prepared. Send out the agenda in advance of the board meeting. Clearly state the purpose, the deliverables, and if you expect them to "do" anything. If you don't ask, they won't know how they can help you.

Respect Time. To volunteers, time is their most valuable asset. Start on time. End on time. Where possible, ask them to review summary materials (not the whole enchilada — unless they ask for it) prior to attending the session.

Be Flexible around schedules and special needs. Your volunteers are, after all, helping the cause. But, if you find yourself bending way over backwards, they are hindering forward movement. You may need to reconsider their participation.

Provide Social Opportunities. Volunteers also participate because of the networking and social opportunities. Encourage members to arrive early or stay late to socialize, but get down to business during the actual meeting.

Recognize Effort. Your lavish praise may be the only reason they keep coming back. Be creative in finding new ways to tell them how much you appreciate their help and support through thank-you notes, newsletter photos, and the spoken "thank you," not just once, but often.

If volunteers know that they are in good hands and appreciated, they will be more likely to show up and do great work.

Chapter Nine

Golden Nuggets

Whenever I finish reading a book, listening to a speech, or taking a course, I always ask myself "so what?" What are the "golden nuggets" or key ideas, themes or actions that will make a difference *for me*?

Everyone who reads this book, or even glances through it, will pick up something different. What are *your* golden nuggets or key ideas that will make a difference *for you*?

Key Themes

- ❑ Have a business reason for working together as a team.

- ❑ Set your team up for success with a charter.

- ❑ Have the right people on the team.

- ❑ Plan for success at every session.

- ❑ Agree to some basic team rules:

    - ❑ Use and follow an agenda.

    - ❑ Establish and review team ground rules.

    - ❑ Share the wealth by sharing roles.

    - ❑ Agree on the process to generate, organize, decide and take action.

    - ❑ Keep a team memory.

    - ❑ Draft your next team agenda before you leave.

    - ❑ Critique your session to improve your teamwork.

- ❑ All participate. No one dominates.

- ❑ Be considerate and respect each other.

- ❑ Genuinely work together to achieve results.

- ❑ When there is a problem, intervene gracefully — before it gets out of control.

- ❑ Recognize and celebrate small successes.

Appendix

Additional Resources on Teams

Team Basics is certainly not the definitive source on teams. This book highlights the most important items you need to know to get started. I have focused on the "what" you need to know and the "how" to do it — so you can hit the deck running.

It's up to you to continue learning more about teams. The more you work with teams, the more you will want to know why teams work the way they do.

This appendix provides a partial list of some of the better and more comprehensive books on teamwork.

Blanchard, Kenneth, Ph.D., et al. *The One Minute Manager Builds High Performing Teams*. New York: William Morrow and Company, Inc., 1990. ISBN 0-688-10972-1.

Covey, Stephen R. *The Seven Habits of Highly Effective People*. New York: Simon and Schuster, 1989. ISBN 0-671-66398-4.

Daniels, William R. *Orchestrating Powerful Regular Meetings: A Manager's Complete Guide*. San Diego: Pfeiffer & Company, 1990. ISBN 0-89384-231-1.

Dee, David. *First Team*. The Dartnell Corporation, 1995. ISBN 0-85013-234-7.

Doyle, Michael, and David Straus. *How To Make Meetings Work*. New York: The Berkley Publishing Group, 1982. ISBN 0-515-09048-4.

Fisher, Kimball, et al. *Tips For Teams: A Ready Reference for Solving Common Team Problems*. New York: Belgard, Fisher, Rayner, Inc., 1995. ISBN 0-07-021167-1.

Henry, Jane E., Ph.D. and Meg Hartzler. *Tools for Virtual Teams: A Team Fitness Companion*. Milwaukee: ASQ Quality Press, 1998. ISBN 0-87389-381-6.

Katzenbach, Jon R. and Douglas K. Smith. *The Wisdom of Teams: Creating The High-Performance Organization*. Boston: Harvard Business School Press, 1993. ISBN 0-87584-367-0.

Kayser, Thomas A. *Mining Group Gold*. El Segundo: Serif Publishing, 1990. ISBN 1-878567-02-0.

Kostner, Jaclyn. *Knights of the TeleRound Table*. New York: Warner Books, Inc., 1994. ISBN 0-446-51879-4.

Lindborg, Henry J. *The Basics of Cross-Functional Teams*. New York: Quality Resources, 1997. ISBN 0-527-76332-2.

Lipnack, Jessica and Jeffrey Stamps. *Virtual Teams: Reaching Across Space, Time, and Organizations with Technology.* Canada: John Wiley & Sons, Inc. 1997. ISBN 0-471-16553-0.

McDermott, Lynda C., et al. *World Class Teams: Working Across Borders.* Canada: John Wiley & Sons, Inc., 1998. ISBN 0-471-29265-6.

Mohrman, Susan Albers, et al. *Designing Team-Based Organizations.* San Francisco: Jossey-Bass Inc., 1995. ISBN 0-7879-0800-X.

Morrisey, George L. *Morrisey on Planning: A Guide to Strategic Thinking: Building Your Planning Foundation.* San Francisco: Jossey-Bass Inc., 1996. ISBN 0-7879-0168-7.

Morrisey, George L. *Morrisey on Planning: A Guide to Long Range Planning: Creating Your Strategic Journey.* San Francisco: Jossey-Bass Inc., 1996. ISBN 0-7879-0169-5.

Organizational Dynamics, Inc. *Making Teams Work: A Guide to Creating and Managing Teams.* Burlington: Organizational Dynamics, Inc., 1993. 0-9636723-0-4.

Rees, Fran. *10 Steps to Results: Teamwork from Start to Finish.* San Francisco: Jossey-Bass/Pfeiffer, 1997. ISBN 0-7879-1061-9.

Scholtes, Peter R., et al. *The Team Handbook.* Madison: Joiner Associates, Inc., 1988. ISBN 0-9622264-0-8.

Varney, Glenn H. *Building Productive Teams: An Action Guide and Resource Book.* San Francisco: Jossey Bass Inc., 1989. ISBN 1-55542-180-6.

Index

About the Author

Kristin J. Arnold, CPCM helps corporations, government and non-profit organizations achieve extraordinary results. With years of team-building and facilitation experience, Kristin specializes in coaching executives and their leadership, management and employee teams to be *extraordinary.*

In addition to facilitation services, QPC Inc. offers diversified programs around the team concept to meet the needs of CEOs, COOs, executives, managers and team members. Her highly customized speeches and seminars have become instrumental in achieving higher performance and exceptional results within the workplace.

❑   Extraordinary Teams Produce Extraordinary Results

❑   Wild Teams: The Hottest Trends in Teamwork

❑   Teams Aren't for Everyone

❑   Boomers and Xers — Bridging the Generations

❑   Technology to Leverage Your Teamwork

❑   The Extraordinary Team Facilitator

An accomplished author and editor of several professional articles, books and audiocassette tapes, as well as a featured columnist in *The Daily Press,* Kristin is regarded as an expert in team development, facilitation and process improvement techniques.

For more information on how Kristin can help your teams become extraordinary, contact her at:

Quality Process Consultants, Inc.
48 West Queens Way
Hampton, Virginia 23669
(757) 728.0191 or 800.589.4733
FAX: (757) 728.0192
www.qpcteam.com